Berlitz®

Turkis

phrase book & dictionary

Berlitz Publishing
New York   London   Singapore

Contents

Food & Drink

People

Leisure Time

Special Requirements

In an Emergency

Dictionary

Pronunciation

This section is designed to familiarize you with the sounds of Turkish using our simplified phonetic transcription. You'll find the pronunciation of the Turkish letters explained below, together with their 'imitated' equivalents. To use this system, found throughout the phrase book, simply read the pronunciation as if it were English, noting any special rules below.

Letters underlined in the transcriptions should be read with slightly more stress, but don't overdo this as Turkish is not a heavily stressed language.

Consonants

Letter	Approximate Pronunciation	Symbol	Example	Pronunciation
c	like j in jam	j	**ceket**	*jeh•keht*
ç	like ch in church	ch	**kaç**	*kahch*
g	like g in ground	g	**gitmek**	*geet•mehk*
ğ	1. at the end of a word, it lengthens the preceding vowel		**dağ**	*dah**
	2. a silent letter between vowels		**kağıt**	*kah•iht*
	3. after e, like y in yawn	y	**değer**	*deh•yehr*
h	like h in hit	h	**mahkeme**	*mah•keh•meh*
j	like s in pleasure	zh	**bagaj**	*bah•gahzh*
r	trilled r	r	**tren**	*trehn*
s	like s in sit	s	**siyah**	*see•yahh*
ş	like sh in shut	sh	**şişe**	*shee•sheh*

Letters b, d, f, k, l, m, n, p, t, v, y and z are pronounced as in English.

*Bold indicates a lengthening of the sound, an extra emphasis on the vowel sound.

Turkish consonants are typically shorter and harder-sounding than English consonants. When reading Turkish words, be sure to pronounce all the letters.

Vowels

Letter	Approximate Pronunciation	Symbol	Example	Pronunciation
a	like a in father	ah	kara	kah•rah
e	like e in net	eh	sene	seh•neh
ı	similar to i in ill	ih	tatlı	taht•lih
i	like ee in see	ee	sim	seem
o	like o in spot	oh	otel	oh•tehl
ö	similar to ur in fur	ur	börek	bur•rehk
u	like oo in cool	oo	uzak	oo•zahk
ü	like ew in few	yu	üç	yuch

Turkish vowels are quite different from English vowels. As with consonants, they are generally shorter and harder than English vowels. In the pronunciation guide, certain vowels are followed by an 'h' to emphasize the shortness of the sound.

Diphthongs

Letter	Approximate Pronunciation	Symbol	Example	Pronunciation
ay	like ie in tie	**ie**	**bay**	*bie*
ey	like ay in day	**ay**	**bey**	*bay*
oy	like oy in boy	**oy**	**koy**	*koy*

Türkçe (Turkish) is the native language of some 70 million inhabitants of the Republic of Turkey, and is spoken by large numbers of ethnic Turks living outside of Turkey. The Turkish alphabet used today dates only from 1928, when Atatürk, the founder of Modern Turkey, chose to replace the Ottoman script that had been used for centuries.

Turkish differs from English in two important ways. First, affixes take the place of many words that, in other languages, would be written separately (such as pronouns, negatives and prepositions); these affixes are attached to a base word. Second, it features 'vowel harmony'; this restricts which vowels may appear within a word. So, while affixes in their standard forms have the vowel 'i' or 'e', this may change when the affix is attached to another word. For example, the suffix **in** (´s) stays **in** in **evin** (the house's), but becomes **un** in **memurun** (the official's) and **ün** in **gözün** (the eye's).

How to use this Book

Sometimes you see two alternatives in italics, separated by a slash. Choose the one that's right for your situation.

ESSENTIAL

A one-way [single]/
round-trip [return] ticket.

Sadece gidiş/gidiş dönüş bileti.
sah•deh•jeh gee•deesh/gee•deesh
dur•nyush bee•leh•tee

How much?
Are there any discounts?

Ne kadar? *neh kah•dahr*
İndirim var mı? *een•dee•reem vahr mih*

Words you may see are shown in YOU MAY SEE boxes.

YOU MAY SEE...

PERONLARA — to the platforms
DANIŞMA — information
YER AYIRTMA — reservations

Any of the words or phrases listed can be plugged into the sentence below.

Train

Where is/are...? **...nerede?** *...neh•reh•deh*
  the ticket office **Bilet gişesi** *bee•leht gee•sheh•see*
  the information desk **Danışma masası** *dah•nihsh•mah*
    mah•sah•sih

  the luggage lockers **Bagaj dolapları** *bah•gahj doh•lahp•lah•rih*

Turkish phrases appear in purple.

Read the simplified pronunciation as if it were English. For more on pronunciation, see page 7.

Tickets

When's…to Istanbul? **İstanbul'a…ne zaman?** *ees·tahn·boo·lah …neh zah·mahn*

the (first) bus **(ilk) otobüs** *(eelk) oh·toh·byus*

the (next) flight **(bundan sonraki) uçak** *(boon·dahn sohn·rah·kee) oo·chahk*

the (last) train **(son) tren** *(sohn) trehn*

For Numbers, see page 176.

Related phrases can be found by going to the page number indicated.

Cash can be obtained from **paramatik** (ATMs), which are located throughout Turkey. Some debit cards and most major credit cards are accepted. Be sure you know your PIN and whether it is compatible with Turkish machines. ATMs offer good rates, though there may be some hidden fees.

Information boxes contain relevant country, culture and language tips.

Expressions you may hear are shown in You May Hear boxes.

YOU MAY HEAR…

Lütfen, biletiniz/pasaportunuz. *lyut·fehn bee·leh·tee·neez/pah·sah·por·too·nooz* Your ticket/passport, please.

Color-coded side bars identify each section of the book.

Survival

Arrival & Departure

ESSENTIAL

I'm here on vacation [holiday]/business.
Tatil/İş için buradayım. *tah·teel/eesh ee·cheen boo·rah·dah·yihm*

I'm going to...
...gidiyorum. *...gee·dee·yoh·room*

I'm staying at the...Hotel.
...otelinde kalıyorum. *...oh·teh·leen·deh kah·lih·yoh·room*

YOU MAY HEAR...

Lütfen, biletiniz/pasaportunuz. *lyut·fehn bee·leh·tee·neez/pah·sah·pohr·too·nooz*
Your ticket/passport please.

Ziyaret sebebiniz nedir? *zee·yah·reht seh·beh·bee·neez neh·deer*
What's the purpose of your visit?

Nerede kalıyorsunuz? *neh·reh·deh kah·lih·yohr·soo·nooz*
Where are you staying?

Ne kadar kalacaksınız? *neh kah·dahr kah·lah·jak·sih·nihz*
How long are you staying?

Kiminlesiniz? *kee·meen·leh·see·neez*
Who are you with?

Border Control

I'm just passing through.
Sadece geçiyorum. *sah·deh·jeh geh·chee·yoh·room*

I would like to declare...
...beyan etmek istiyorum. *...beh·yahn eht·mehk ees·tee·yoh·room*

I have nothing to declare.
Beyan edeceğim birşey yok. *beh·yahn eh·deh·jeh·yeem beer shay yohk*

YOU MAY HEAR...

Gümrüğe tabi eşyanız var mı?
gyum•ryu•yeh tah•bee ehsh•yah•nihz vahr mih

Do you have anything to declare?

Bunun için gümrük vergisi ödemeniz gerekir. *boo•noon ee•cheen gyum•ryuk vehr•gee•see ur•deh•meh•neez geh•reh•keer*

You must pay duty on this.

Lütfen şu çantayı açınız. *lyut•fehn shoo chahn•tah•yih ah•chih•nihz*

Please open that bag.

YOU MAY SEE...

GÜMRÜK	customs
VERGİSİZ EŞYALAR	duty-free goods
BEYAN EDECEK EŞYASI OLANLAR	passengers with goods to declare
BEYAN EDECEK EŞYASI OLMAYANLAR	passengers with nothing to declare
PASAPORT KONTROLU	passport control
POLİS	police

Money

ESSENTIAL

Where's…?	**…nerede?** …_neh_•reh•deh
the ATM	**Paramatik** pah•rah•mah•_teek_
the bank	**Banka** _bahn_•kah
the currency exchange office	**Döviz bürosu** dur•_veez_ byu•roh•soo
What time does the bank open/close?	**Banka saat kaçta açılıyor/kapanıyor?** _bahn_•kah sah•aht kach•_tah_ ah•chih•_lih_•yohr/kah•pah•_nih_•yohr
I'd like to change dollars/pounds into lira.	**Dolar/İngiliz Sterlini bozdurmak istiyorum.** doh•_lahr_/een•gee•leez stehr•lee•_nee_ bohz•door•_mahk_ ees•_tee_•yoh•room
I want to cash some traveler's checks [cheques].	**Seyahat çekleri bozdurmak istiyorum.** seh•yah•_haht_ chek•leh•_ree_ bohz•door•_mahk_ ees•_tee_•yoh•room

At the Bank

Can I exchange foreign currency here?	**Burada döviz bozdurabilir miyim?** _boo·rah·dah dur·veez bohz·doo·rah·bee·leer mee·yeem_
What's the exchange rate?	**Döviz kuru nedir?** _dur·veez koo·roo neh·deer_

At some banks, cash can be obtained from ATMs with Visa™, Eurocard™, American Express® and many other international cards. Instructions are often given in English. Banks with a **Change** sign will exchange foreign currency. You can also change money at travel agencies and hotels, but the rate will not be as good. Remember to bring your passport when you want to change money.

YOU MAY SEE...

The monetary unit is the Turkish Lira (**Türk Lirasi,** abbreviated **TL**.) One **TL** is divided into one hundred **yeni kuruş**, abbreviated **Kr**.
Coins: 1, 5, 10, 25, 50 **Kr** and **1 TL**
Notes: 5, 10, 20, 50 and 100 **TL**

YOU MAY SEE...

KARTI TAK	insert card
İPTAL ET	cancel
SİL	clear
GİR	enter
PİN NUMARASI	PIN
ÇEKİLEN PARALAR	withdraw funds
CARİ HESAPTAN	from checking [current] account
TASARRUF HESABINDAN	from savings account
FATURA	receipt

Banka (the bank) and **postahane** (the post office) are good options for exchanging currency. **Döviz bürosu** (currency exchange offices) are also located in many tourist centers, though if you decide to change money in an exchange office, look around for the best rate and keep your eye on the commission. Also, remember to bring your passport, in case you are asked for identification.

How much is the fee?	**Ne kadar komisyon alıyorsunuz?** _neh kah·dahr koh·mees·yohn ah·lih·yohr·soo·nooz_
I've lost my traveler's checks [cheques].	**Seyahat çeklerimi kaybettim.** _seh·yah·haht chehk·leh·ree·mee kie·beht·teem_
My credit card was lost.	**Kredi kartım kayboldu.** _kreh·dee kahr·tihm kie·bohl·doo_
My credit cards have been stolen.	**Kredi kartlarım çalındı.** _kreh·dee kahrt·lah·rihm chah·lihn·dih_
My card doesn't work.	**Kartım çalışmıyor.** _kahr·tihm chah·lihsh·mih·yohr_

For Numbers, see page 176.

Getting Around

ESSENTIAL

How do I get to town?	**Şehire nasıl gidebilirim?** *sheh•hee•reh nah•sıhl gee•deh•bee•lee•reem*
Where's...?	**...nerede?** *...neh•reh•deh*
the airport	**Havaalanı** *hah•vah•ah•lah•nıh*
the train [railway] station	**Tren garı** *trehn gah•rih*
the bus station	**Otobüs garajı** *oh•toh•byus gah•rah•jih*
the subway [underground] station	**Metro istasyonu** *meht•roh ees•tahs•yoh•noo*
How far is it?	**Ne kadar uzakta?** *neh kah•dahr oo•zahk•tah*
Where can I buy tickets?	**Nereden bilet alabilirim?** *neh•reh•dehn bee•leht ah•lah•bee•lee•reem*
A one-way [single]/ round-trip [return] ticket.	**Sadece gidiş/gidiş dönüş bileti.** *sah•deh•jeh gee•deesh/gee•deesh dur•nyush bee•leh•tee*
How much?	**Ne kadar?** *neh kah•dahr*
Are there any discounts?	**İndirim var mı?** *een•dee•reem vahr mih*
Which...?	**Hangi...?** *hahn•gee...*
gate?	**kapı?** *kah•pih*
lane?	**hat?** *haht*
platform?	**peron?** *peh•rohn*
Where can I get a taxi?	**Nerede taksi bulabilirim?** *neh•reh•deh tahk•see boo•lah•bee•lee•reem*
Please take me to this address.	**Lütfen beni bu adrese götürün.** *lyut•fehn beh•nee boo ahd•reh•seh gur•tyu•ryun*

18

Where can I rent a car?	**Nereden bir araba kiralayabilirim?** _neh•reh•dehn_ beer ah•rah•_bah_ kee•rah•lah•yah•bee•_lee_•reem
Can I have a map?	**Bir harita alabilir miyim?** beer hah•reeh•_tah_ ah•lah•bee•_leer_•mee•yeem

Tickets

When's…to Istanbul?	**İstanbul'a…ne zaman?** ees•_tahn_•boo•lah…_neh_ zah•mahn
the (first) bus	**(ilk) otobüs** (eelk) oh•toh•_byus_
the (next) flight	**(bundan sonraki) uçak** (boon•_dahn_ sohn•rah•kee) oo•_chahk_
the (last) train	**(son) tren** (sohn) trehn
Where can I buy tickets?	**Nereden bilet alabilirim?** _neh_•reh•dehn bee•_leht_ ah•lah•bee•_lee_•reem
One ticket/two tickets, please.	**Bir/İki bilet lütfen.** beer/ee•_kee_ bee•_leht_ _lyut_•fehn
For today/tomorrow.	**Bugün/Yarın.** _boo_•gyun/_yah_•rihn
A one-way [single]/ return ticket.	**Sadece gidiş/gidiş dönüş bileti.** _sah_•deh•jeh gee•_deesh_/gee•_deesh_ dur•_nyush_ bee•leh•tee
A first/economy class ticket.	**Birinci sınıf/Ekonomi sınıfı bileti.** bee•reen•_jee_ sih•_nihf_/eh•koh•noh•_mee_ sih•nih•_fih_ bee•leh•tee

How much?	**Ne kadar?** <u>neh</u> kah·dahr
Is there a discount for…?	**…için indirim var mı?** … ee·<u>cheen</u> een·dee·<u>reem</u> vahr mih
children	**Çocuklar** choh·jook·<u>lahr</u>
students	**Öğrenciler** ur·rehn·jee·<u>lehr</u>
senior citizens	**Yaşlılar** yash·lih·<u>lahr</u>
I have an e-ticket.	**Bir e-biletim var.** beer eh·bee·leh·teem vahr
Can I buy a ticket on the bus/train?	**Otobüste/Trende bir bilet alabilir miyim?** oh·toh·byu·<u>steh</u>/trehn·<u>deh</u> beer bee·<u>leht</u> ah·lah·bee·<u>leer</u>·mee·yeem
Can I return on the same ticket?	**Aynı biletle dönebilir miyim?** ie·nih bee·leht·leh dur·nee·bee·leer mee·yeem?
I'd like to…my reservation.	**Reservasyonumu…istiyorum.** reh·zehr·vahs·yoh·noo·<u>moo</u>…ees·tee·yoh·room
cancel	**iptal etmek** eep·<u>tahl</u> eht·<u>mehk</u>
change	**değiştirmek** deh·yeesh·teer·<u>mehk</u>
confirm	**teyit etmek** teh·<u>yeet</u> eht·<u>mehk</u>
Do I have to stamp the ticket before boarding?	**Binmeden önce biletimi mühürletmem gerekiyor mu?** been·meh·dehn ohn·jeh bee·leh·tee·mih myu·huhr·leht·mehm geh·reh·kee·yohr·moo?

How long is this ticket valid?	**Bilet ne kadar zaman geçerli?** *bee·leht neh kah·dahr zah·mahn geh·chehr·lee?*

For Days, see page 178.

For Time, see page 177.

YOU MAY HEAR…

Hangi havayoluyla uçuyorsunuz? *hahn·gee hah·vah yoh·looy·lah oo·choo·yohr·soo·nooz*	What airline are you flying?
İç/Dış hatlar mı? *eech/dihsh haht·lahr mih*	Domestic/International?
Hangi terminal? *hahn·gee tehr·mee·nahl*	What terminal?

Plane

Airport Transfer

How much is a taxi to the airport?	**Havaalanına bir taksi ne kadar?** *hah·vah·ah·lah·nih·nah beer tahk·see neh kah·dahr*
To…Airport, please.	**…havaalanına lütfen.** *…hah·vah·ah·lah·nih·nah lyut·fehn*
My airline is…	**Havayolum…** *hah·vah·yoh·loom…*
My flight leaves at…	**Uçağım saat…kalkacak.** *oo·chah·ihm sah·aht… kahl·kah·jahk*
I'm in a rush.	**Acelem var.** *ah·jeh·lehm vahr*
Can you take an alternate route?	**Alternatif bir yol kullanabilir misiniz?** *ahl·tehr·nah·teef beer yohl kool·lah·nah·bee·leer·mee·see·neez*
Can you drive faster/ slower?	**Daha hızlı/yavaş kullanabilir misiniz?** *dah·hah hihz·lih/yah·vash kool·lah·nah·bee·leer·mee·see·neez*

YOU MAY HEAR...

Bir sonraki! *beer sohn·rah·_kee_** — Next!

Lütfen, biletiniz/pasaportunuz. *_lyut_·fehn bee·leh·tee·_neez_/pah·sah·pohr·too·_nooz_* — Your ticket/passport, please.

Kaç parça bavulunuz var? *_kach_ pahr·_chah_ bah·voo·loo·_nooz_ vahr* — How much luggage do you have?

Bavul ağırlığınız fazla. *bah·_vool_ ah·ihr·lih·ih·_nihz_ fahz·_lah_* — You have excess luggage.

El çantası için o çok ağır/büyük. *ehl chahn·tah·_sih_ ee·_cheen_ oh chohk ah·_ihr_/byu·_yuhk_* — That's too heavy/large for a carry-on [to carry on board].

Bu çantaları kendiniz mi hazırladınız? *boo chan·tah·lah·_rih_ kehn·dee·_neez_ mee hah·zihr· lah·dih·_nihz_* — Did you pack these bags yourself?

Taşımanız için herhangi bir şey verildi mi? *tah·shih·mah·_nihz_ ee·_cheen_ hehr·_hahn_·gee beer _shay_ veh·reel·_dee_ mee* — Did anyone give you anything to carry?

Ceplerinizi boşaltın. *jehp·leh·ree·nee·_zee_ boh·_shahl_·tihn* — Empty your pockets.

Ayakkabılarınızı çıkarın. *ah·yahk·kah·bih·lah·rih·nih·_zih_ chih·_kah_·rihn* — Take off your shoes.

Şu anda kalkan uçak... *shoo ahn·_dah_ kahl·_kahn_ oo·_chahk_...* — Now boarding flight...

Checking In

Where is check-in?	**Kayıt masası nerede?** *kah·yiht mah·sah·sih neh·reh·deh*
My name is…	**İsmim…** *ees·meem…*
I'm going to…	**…gidiyorum.** *…gee·dee·yoh·room*
I have…	
one suitcase	**Bir tane bavulum var** *beer tah·neh bah·voo· bah·voo· loom vahr*
two suitcases	**İki tane bavulum var** *ee·kee tah·neh bah·voo·loom vahr*
one piece of hand luggage	**Bir tane el bagajım var beer** *tah·neh ehl bah·gah·zhihm vahr*
How much luggage is allowed?	**Ne kadar bavula izin var?** *neh kah·dahr bah·voo·lah ee·zeen vahr*
Which gate does flight…leave from?	**…numaralı uçak hangi biniş kapısından hareket edecek?** *…noo·mah·rah·lih oo·chahk hahn·gee bee·neesh kah·pih·sihn·dahn hah·reh·keht eh·deh·jehk*
I'd like a window/an aisle seat.	**Pencere/Koridor kenarı istiyorum.** *pehn·jeh·reh/ koh·ree·dor keh·nah·rih ees·tee·yoh·room*

When do we leave/ arrive?	**Ne zaman ayrılıyoruz/varıyoruz?** *neh zah•man ie•rih•lih•yoh•rooz/vah•rih•yoh•rooz*
Is there any delay on flight…?	**…uçuşunda herhangi bir gecikme var mı?** *… oo•choo•shoon•dah hehr•hahn•gee beer geh•jeek•meh vahr mih*
How late will it be?	**Ne kadar gecikecek?** *neh kah•dahr geh•jee•keh•jehk*

YOU MAY SEE…

VARIŞ	arrivals
GİDİŞ	departures
BAVUL TESLİM BANDI	baggage claim
İÇ HAT UÇUŞLARI	domestic flights
DIŞ HAT UÇUŞLARI	international flights
UÇUŞ KAYDI MASASI	check-in desk
E-BİLET KAYDI	e-ticket check-in
ÇIKIŞ KAPILARI	departure gates

Luggage

Where is/are…?	**…nerede?** _neh•reh•deh_
the luggage carts [trolleys]	**El arabaları** _ehl ah•rah•bah•lah•rih_
the luggage lockers	**Bagaj dolapları** _bah•gahj doh•lahp•lah•rih_
the baggage claim	**Bavul teslim bandı** _bah•vool tehs•leem bahn•dih_
My luggage has been lost.	**Bavulumu kaybettim.** _bah•voo•loo•moo kie•beht•teem_
My luggage has been stolen.	**Bavulum çalındı.** _bah•voo•loom chah•lihn•dih_
My suitcase was damaged.	**Bavulum hasar görmüş.** _bah•voo•loom hah•sahr gurr•myush_

Finding your Way

Where is/are…?	**…nerede?** _neh•reh•deh_
the currency exchange office	**Döviz bürosu** _dur•veez byu•roh•soo_
the car rental	**Araba kiralama** _ah•rah•bah kee•rah•lah•mah_
the exit	**Çıkış** _chih•kihsh_
the taxis	**Taksiler** _tahk•see•lehr_
Is there…into town?	**Kente…var mı?** _kehn•teh…vahr mih_
a bus	**otobüs** _oh•toh•byus_
a train	**tren** _trehn_
a Metro	**metro** _meht•roh_

For Directions, see page 36.

YOU MAY SEE...

PERONLARA	to the platforms
DANIŞMA	information
YER AYIRTMA	reservations
VARIŞ	arrivals
ÇIKIŞ	departures

Train

How do I get to the train station?	**Tren garına nasıl gidebilirim?** *trehn gah·rih·nah nah·sihl gee·deh·bee·lee·reem*
Is it far?	**Uzak mı?** *oo·zahk mih*
Where is/are...?	**...nerede?** ...*neh·reh·deh*
the ticket office	**Bilet gişesi** *bee·leht gee·sheh·see*
the luggage lockers	**Bagaj dolapları** *bah·gahj doh·lahp·lah·rih*
the platforms	**Peronlar** *peh·rohn·lahr*
Could I have a schedule [timetable], please?	**Lütfen, bir tren tarifesi alabilir miyim?** *lyut·fehn beer trehn tah·ree·feh·see ah·lah·bee·leer mee·yeem*

YOU MAY HEAR...

Lütfen yerlerinizi alın! *lyut·fehn yehr·leh·ree·nee·zee ah·lihn*	All aboard!
Biletler lütfen. *bee·leht·lehr lyut·fehn*	Tickets, please.
...aktarma yapmanız gerek. ...*ahk·tahr·mah yahp·mah·nihz geh·rehk*	You have to change at...
Bir sonraki durak... *beer sohn·rah·kee doo·rahk...*	Next stop...

The **Türkiye Cumhuriyeti Devlet Demiryolları (TCDD)**
(Turkish Republic State Railways) operates in most regions of
the country. Trains with sleeping cars are a good option for a long,
overnight trip. For international travel, there are a number of express
trains with separate first- and second-class cars. The cost of tickets for
each differs by about 30%. For reduced rates on international travel,
purchase an InterRail pass or a Balkan Flexipass. For domestic travel, be
sure to inquire about train stops. Express trains generally connect large
cities, while commuter trains are slower and make various stops along
the route. Reservations may be made in advance via the TCDD website.

How long is the trip?	**Yolculuk ne kadar sürüyor?** *yohl·joo·look neh kah·dahr syu·ryu·yohr*
Do I have to change trains?	**Aktarma yapmak gerekiyor mu?** *ahk·tahr·mah yahp·mahk geh·reh·kee·yohr moo*

For Asking Directions, see page 36.

For Tickets, see page 19.

Departures

Which platform does the train to…leave from?	**…giden tren hangi perondan kalkıyor?** …*gee·dehn trehn hahn·gee peh·rohn·dahn kahl·kih·yohr*
Is this the platform to…?	**…treni bu perondan mı kalkıyor?** …*treh·nee boo peh·rohn·dahn mih kahl·kih·yohr*
Where is platform…?	**…peronu nerede?** …*peh·roh·noo neh·reh·deh*
Where do I change for…?	**…için nerede aktarma yapacağım?** …*ee·cheen neh·reh·deh ahk·tahr·mah yah·pah·jah·yihm*

On Board

Is this seat taken?	**Bu koltuk dolu mu?** *boo kohl·took doh·loo moo*
I think that's my seat.	**Bu koltuk benim.** *boo kohl·took beh·neem*
Here's my reservation.	**Buyrun rezervasyonum.** *booy·roon reh·zehr·vahs·yoh·noom*

Bus

Where's the bus station?	**Otobüs garajı nerede?** *oh·toh·byus gah·rah·jih neh·reh·deh*
How far is it?	**Ne kadar uzakta?** *neh kah·dahr oo·zahk·tah*
How do I get to…?	**…nasıl gidebilirim?** …*nah·sihl gee·deh·bee·lee·reem*

Turkish city buses are very inexpensive. Destinations are usually posted on the bus itself, but double check with the driver before boarding. In Istanbul, green buses are reserved for commuters and require payment in special tokens. Orange buses are public and tickets can be purchased on board. In Istanbul, it is a good idea to purchase an **akbil** (smart ticket) which allows you to buy credit to pay for bus, sea and subway/tunnel travel. Paying with an **akbil** gets you a discount of between 10-25%.

Does the bus stop at…?	**Otobüs…duruyor mu?**	*oh·toh·byus…* *doo·roo·yohr moo*
Could you tell me when to get off?	**İneceğim yeri söyler misiniz?**	*ee·neh·jeh·yeem yeh·ree sur·ylehr mee·see·neez*
Do I have to change buses?	**Aktarma yapmam gerekiyor mu?**	*ahk·tahr·mah yahp·mahm geh·reh·kee·yohr moo*
Stop here, please!	**Burada durun lütfen!**	*boo·rah·dah doo·roon lyut·fehn*

For Tickets, see page 19.

YOU MAY SEE…

OTOBÜS DURAĞI	bus stop
GİRİŞ/ÇIKIŞ	enter/exit
BİLETİNİZİ MÜHÜRLETİN	stamp your ticket

Metro transportation is an option in Ankara and Istanbul. **Tünel** (Tunnel), the second-oldest metro in the world, first used in 1875, is located in Istanbul and travels between the Karaköy and Beyoğlu stations. Paying by **akbil** (smart ticket) will get you a discount on both metro and Tünel travel in Istanbul.

Metro

Where's the metro station?	**En yakın metro istasyonu nerede?** *ehn yah·kihn meht·roh ees·tah·syoh·noo neh·reh·deh*
Can I have a map of the metro?	**Bir metro planı verir misiniz?** *beer meht·roh plah·nih veh·reer mee·see·neez*
Which line for...?	**...için hangi hattı kullanmam gerekiyor?** *...ee·cheen hahn·gee haht·tih kool·lahn·mahm geh·reh·kee·yohr*
Where do I change for...?	**...gitmek için nerede tren değiştirmeliyim?** *...geet·mehk ee·cheen neh·reh·deh trehn deh·yeesh·teer·meh·lee·yeem*
Is this the right train for...?	**Bu tren...gidiyor mu?** *boo trehn... gee·dee·yohr moo*
How many stops to...?	**...kaç durak var?** *kach doo·rahk vahr?*
Where are we?	**Neredeyiz?** *neh·reh·deh·yeez*

For Tickets, see page 19.

Boat & Ferry

When is the ferry to...?	**...araba vapuru saat kaçta?** *...ah·rah·bah vah·poo·roo sah·aht kahch·tah*
Where are the life jackets?	**Can yelekleri neredeler?** *jahn yeh·lehk·leh·ree neh·reh·deh·ler?*

YOU MAY SEE...

CANKURTARAN SANDALI	life boats
CAN YELEĞİ	life jackets

Turkey is essentially surrounded by water. That, combined with Turkey's habitual road traffic, makes boat travel an important alternative. The country's most important port is in Istanbul. **İstanbul Deniz Otobüsleri (IDO)** (Istanbul Sea Bus Company) provides regular catamaran and ferry service around Istanbul. Catamarans are generally more comfortable and faster, though it is more expensive to take a catamaran than a ferry. **Denizline** operates between Istanbul and Izmir and a number of operators provide ferry and car ferry service between Çesme and Brindisi and Ancona, Italy. There are also a number of connections between Turkey and the Aegean Islands in summertime. **Akbil** (smart ticket) can also be used for sea travel, giving you a discount of between 10-25% on your travel.

What time is the next sailing?	**Bir sonraki sefer saat kaçta?** *beer sohn ·rah ·kee seh ·fehr sah·aht kach ·tah*
Can I book a seat/cabin?	**Bir yer/kabin ayırtabilir miyim?** *beer yehr/ kah·been ah ·yihr·tah ·bee ·leer mee ·yeem*
How long is the crossing?	**Sefer ne kadar sürüyor?** *seh·fehr neh kah·dahr syu·ryu·yohr*

Taxi

Where can I get a taxi?	**Nerede taksi bulabilirim?** <u>neh</u>·reh·deh tahk·<u>see</u> boo·lah·bee·<u>lee</u>·reem
I'd like a taxi now/for tomorrow at...	**Şimdi/Yarın saat...için bir taksi istiyorum.** <u>sheem</u>·dee/yah·<u>rihn</u> sah·<u>aht</u>...ee·<u>cheen</u> beer tahk·<u>see</u> ees·<u>tee</u>·yoh·room
Can you send a taxi?	**Bir taksi yollayabilir misiniz?** beer tahk·see yol·lah·yah·bee·leer mee·see·neez
Pick me up at....	**Beni...al.** beh·<u>nee</u>...<u>teh</u> ahl
Please take me to...	**Beni...götürür müsünüz lütfen.** beh·<u>nee</u>... gur·tyu·<u>ryur</u> myu·syu·nyuz <u>lyut</u>·fehn
this address	**bu adrese** boo ahd·reh·<u>seh</u>
the airport	**havaalanına** hah·<u>vah</u>·ah·lah·nih·<u>nah</u>
the train station	**tren garına** trehn gah·rih·<u>nah</u>

Turkish taxis are generally yellow, marked with the word **taksi** (taxi) on top and have a letter 'T' on their license plates. Make sure that the meter is set to the correct rate: **gündüz** (day), from 6 a.m. to midnight, and **gece** (night), from midnight to 6 a.m. If you want to tip the driver, you can round up the fare. **Dolmuş** (group taxis) are an alternative to regular taxis. They follow specific routes, much like a bus, but stop as requested. They are cheaper than individual taxis.

I'm late.	**Geciktim.** geh·jeek·teem
Can you drive faster/ slower?	**Daha hızlı/yavaş kullanabilir misiniz?** dah·hah hihz·lih/yah·vahsh kool·lah·nah·bee·leer mee·see·neez
Stop/Wait here.	**Burada durun/bekleyin.** boo·rah·dah doo·roon/ behk·leh·yeen
How much will it cost?	**Ne kadar tutar?** neh kah·dahr too·tahr
You said…lira.	**Siz…lira dediniz.** seez…lee·rah deh·dee·neez
Keep the change.	**Üstü kalsın.** yus·tyu kahl·sihn
A receipt, please.	**Fatura lütfen.** fah·too·rah lyut·fehn

For Numbers, see page 176.

YOU MAY HEAR…

Nereye? neh·reh·yeh	Where to?
Adres nedir? ahd·rehs neh·deer	What's the address?

Bicycle & Motorbike

I'd like to rent [hire]...	**Bir...kiralamak istiyorum.** *beer... kee·rah·lah·mahk ees·tee·yoh·room*
a bicycle	**bisiklet** *bee·seek·leht*
a moped	**mopet** *moh·peht*
a motorcycle	**motorsiklet** *moh·tohr·seek·leht*
How much per day/ week?	**Günlüğü/Haftalığı ne kadar?** *gyun·lyu·yu/ hahf·tah·lih·ih neh kah·dahr*
Can I have a helmet/ lock?	**Kask/Kilit alabilir miyim?** *kahsk/kee·leet ah·lah·bee·leer mee·yeem*

Car Hire

Where can I rent [hire] a car?	**Nereden bir araba kiralayabilirim?** *neh·reh·dehn beer ah·rah·bah kee·rah·lah·yah·bee·lee·reem*
I'd like to rent [hire]...	**Bir...kiralamak istiyorum.** *beer... kee·rah·lah·mahk ees·tee·yoh·room*
a 2-/4-door car	**iki/dört kapılı araba** *ee·kee/durrt kah·pih·lih ah·rah·bah*
an automatic car	**otomatik araba** *oh·toh·mah·teek ah·rah·bah*
a car with air conditioning	**klimalı araba** *klee·mah·lih ah·rah·bah*
a car seat	**araba koltuğu** *ah·rah·bah kohl·too·oo*
How much...?	**...ne kadar?** *...neh kah·dahr*
per day/week	**Günlüğü/Haftalığı** *gyun·lyu·yu/hahf·tah·lih·ih*
per kilometer	**Kilometre başına** *kee·loh·meht·reh bah·shih·nah*
for unlimited mileage	**Sınırsız yakıt kullanımı** *sih·nihr·sihz yah·kiht kool·lah·nih·mih*
with insurance	**Sigortalı** *sih·gohr·tah·lih*
Are there any special weekend rates?	**Hafta sonu için indirim var mı?** *hahf·tah soh·noo ee·cheen een·dee·reem vahr mih*

34

YOU MAY HEAR...

Uluslararası sürücü belgeniz var mı?
oo•loos•_lahr_•ah•rah•sih syu•ryu•_jyu_ behl•geh•
neez _vahr_ mih

Do you have an
international
driver's license?

Lütfen pasaportunuz. pas•sah•pohr•too•
nooz _lyut_•fehn

Your passport, please.

Sigorta istiyor musunuz? sih•_gohr_•tah ees•
tee•yohr moo•soo•nooz

Do you want insurance?

...ön ödeme var. ..._urn_ ur•deh•_meh_ vahr

There is a deposit of...

Burasını imzalayınız. boo•rah•sih•_nih_ eem•
zah•_lah_•yih•nihz

Please sign here.

Fuel Station

Where's the fuel station, please?	**Benzin istasyonu nerede lütfen?** *behn·zeen ees·tah·syoh·noo neh·reh·deh lyut·fehn*
Fill it up, please.	**Depoyu doldurun lütfen.** *deh·poh·yoo dohl·doo·roon lyut·fehn*
...liters, please.	**...litre lütfen.** *...lee·treh lyut·fehn*
I'll pay in cash/by credit card.	**Nakit/Kredi kartı ile ödeyeceğim.** *nah·keet/kreh·dee kahr·tih ee·leh ur·deh·yeh·jeh·yeem*

YOU MAY SEE...

NORMAL	regular
SÜPER	premium [super]
DİZEL	diesel

Asking Directions

Is this the right road to...?	**Bu,...giden yol mu?** *boo...gee·dehn yohl moo*
How far is it to...?	**...buradan ne kadar uzakta?** *...boo·rah·dahn neh kah·dahr oo·zahk·tah*

Where's...?	**...nerede?** ..._neh·reh·deh_
...Street	**...caddesi** ..._jahd·deh·see_
this address	**Bu adres** _boo ahd·rehs_
the highway [motorway]	**Otoyol** _oh·toh·yohl_
Can you show me on the map?	**Bana haritada gösterebilir misiniz?** _bah·nah hah·ree·tah·dah gurs·teh·reh·bee·leer mee·see·neez_
I'm lost.	**Kayboldum.** _kie·bohl·doom_

YOU MAY HEAR...

doğru ilerde _doh·roo ee·lehr·deh_	straight ahead
solda _sohl·dah_	on the left
sağda _sah·dah_	on the right
köşede/köşeyi dönünce _kur·sheh·deh/ kur·sheh·yee dur·nyun·jeh_	on/around the corner
karşısında _kahr·shih·sihn·dah_	opposite
arkasında _ahr·kah·sihn·dah_	behind
yanında _yah·nihn·dah_	next to
...sonra ..._sohn·rah_	after...
kuzey/güney _koo·zay/gyu·nay_	north/south
doğu/batı _doh·oo/bah·tih_	east/west
trafik ışıklarında _trah·feek ih·shihk·lah·rihn·dah_	at the traffic light
kavşakta _kahv·shahk·tah_	at the intersection

Parking

Can I park here?	**Buraya park edebilir miyim?** _boo•rah•yah_ pahrk _eh•deh•bee•leer_ mee•yeem
Where is the nearest parking garage/ parking lot [car park]?	**En yakın park yeri/oto park nerede?** ehn yah•_kihn_ _pahrk_ yeh•ree/oh•toh _pahrk_ neh•reh•deh
How much…?	**…ne kadar?** …_neh_ kah•dahr
per hour	**Saatlik** sah•aht•_lihk_
per day	**Günlük** gyun•_lyuk_
for overnight	**Bir gecelik** beer geh•jeh•_leek_

YOU MAY SEE...

🛑	**DUR**	stop
▽	**YOL VER**	yield
⊗	**PARK EDİLMEZ**	no parking
⊖	**GİRİŞ YASAK**	no entry
⬆	**TEK YÖN**	one way
🚸	**YAYA GEÇİDİ**	pedestrian crossing

Breakdown & Repair

My car broke down/ doesn't start.	**Arabam bozuldu/çalışmıyor.** *ah·rah·<u>bahm</u> boh·zool·<u>doo</u>/chah·<u>lihsh</u>·mih·yohr*
Can you fix it?	**Onarabilir misiniz?** *oh·nah·rah·bee·<u>leer</u> mee·see·<u>neez</u>*
When will it be ready?	**Ne zaman hazır olur?** *<u>neh</u> zah·mahn hah·<u>zihr</u> oh·<u>loor</u>*
How much will it cost?	**Ne kadar para tutar?** *<u>neh</u> kah·dahr pah·<u>rah</u> too·<u>tahr</u>*
I have a puncture/ flat tyre	**Lastiğim/tekerim patladı** *lahs·tee·yeem/teh·keh·reem paht·lah·dih*

Accidents

There has been an accident.	**Kaza oldu.** *kah·<u>zah</u> ohl·<u>doo</u>*
Call an ambulance/ the police.	**Ambülans/Polis çağırın.** *ahm·byu·<u>lahns</u>/poh·<u>lees</u> chah·<u>ih</u>·rihn*

Places to Stay

ESSENTIAL

Can you recommend a hotel?	**Bir otel tavsiye edebilir misiniz?** _beer oh·tehl_ _tahv·see·yeh eh·deh·bee·leer·mee·see·neez_
I have a reservation.	**Yer ayırtmıştım.** _yehr ah·yihrt·mihsh·tihm_
My name is…	**İsmim…** _ees·meem…_
Do you have a room…	**…odanız var mı?** _…oh·dah·nihz vahr mih_
for one/two	**Bir/İki kişilik** _beer/ee·kee kee·shee·leek_
with a bathroom	**Banyolu** _bahn·yoh·loo_
with air conditioning	**Klimalı** _klee·mah·lih_
For tonight.	**Bu gecelik.** _boo geh·jeh·leek_
For two nights.	**İki geceliğine.** _ee·kee geh·jeh·lee·yee·neh_
For one week.	**Bir haftalığına.** _beer hahf·tah·lih·ih·nah_
How much?	**Ne kadar?** _neh kah·dahr_
Do you have anything cheaper?	**Daha ucuz yer var mı?** _dah·hah oo·jooz yehr vahr mih_

When's check-out?	**Saat kaçta otelden ayrılmamız gerekiyor?** *sah·aht kahch·tah oh·tehl·dehn ie·rihl·mah·mihz geh·reh·kee·yohr*
Can I leave this in the safe?	**Bunu kasaya koyabilir miyim?** *boo·noo kah·sah·yah koh·yah·bee·leer mee·yeem*
Can I leave my bags?	**Eşyalarımı bırakabilir miyim?** *ehsh·yah·lah·rih·mih bih·rah·kah·bee·leer mee·yeem*
Can I have the bill/ a receipt?	**Fiş/Hesap alabilir miyim?** *feesh/heh·sahp ah·lah·bee·leer mee·yeem*
I'll pay in cash/by credit card.	**Nakit/Kredi kartı ile ödeyeceğim.** *nah·keet/ kreh·dee kahr·tih ee·leh ur·deh·yeh·jeh·yeem*

Somewhere to Stay

Can you recommend…?	**…tavsiye edebilir misiniz?** *tahv·see·yeh eh·deh·bee·leer mee·see·neez*
a hotel	**bir hotel** *beer oh·tehl*
a hostel	**bir pansiyon** *beer pahn·see·yohn*
a campsite	**bir kamp alanı** *beer kahmp ah·lah·nih*
a bed and breakfast	**bir pansiyon** *beer pahn·see·yohn*

A range of hotel choices are available in Turkey. In terms of more traditional options, you may choose to stay in **gençlik yurdu** (youth hostels), **pansiyon** (guest houses) or **otel** (hotels). Turkey, however, also offers a number of more special places to stay such as Ottoman mansions, historic houses, Cappadocian cave dwellings, seaside resorts, etc. If you arrive with nowhere booked, contact the **Turizm Danışma Bürosu** (tourist information offices) and they can help you with reservations.

What is it near?	**Yakınında ne var?** _yah_·kih·nihn·_dah_ _neh_ vahr
How do I get there?	**Oraya nasıl gidebilirim?** oh·rah·yah _nah_·sihl
	gee·deh·bee·_lee_·reem

Otel (hotels) in Turkey are labeled with a government-assigned star system (one to five), which generally refers to the number of amenities offered and not how spectacular the hotel may be. Most double rooms are equipped with two twin beds, so if you want a bed for two, be sure to ask. Also, if you want a hotel with air-conditioning, book one that is three-stars or higher. For a more intimate taste of Turkish life, **pansiyon** (guest houses) offer rented rooms and breakfast is usually included in the price. Note that **gençlik yurdu** (youth hostels) are generally only open to card holders.

At the Hotel

I have a reservation.	**Yer ayırtmıştım.** _yehr_ ah·yihrt·_mihsh_·tihm
My name is...	**İsmim...** ees·_meem_...
Do you have a room...?	**...odanız var mı?** ...oh·dah·_nihz_ _vahr_ mih
with a toilet/shower	**Banyolu/Duşlu** bahn·yoh·_loo_/doosh·_loo_
with air conditioning	**Klimalı** _klee_·mah·lih
that's smoking/	**Sigara içilen/içilmeyen** see·_gah_·rah ee·chee·_lehn_/
non-smoking	ee·_cheel_·meh·yehn
For tonight.	**Bu gecelik.** _boo_ geh·jeh·_leek_
For two nights.	**İki geceliğine.** ee·_kee_ geh·jeh·lee·yee·_neh_
For one week.	**Bir haftalığına.** beer hahf·tah·lih·gih·_nah_
Does the hotel have...?	**Otelde bir...var mı?** oh·_tehl_·deh beer... _vahr_ mih
a computer	**bilgisayar** beel·gee·sah·_yahr_
an elevator [a lift]	**asansör** ah·sahn·_surr_

YOU MAY HEAR...

Lütfen pasaportunuz/kredi kartınız.
*lyut·fehn pas·sah·por·too·nooz/kreh·dee
kahr·tih·nihz*

Your passport/credit card, please.

Bu formu doldurun lütfen. *boo fohr·moo
dohl·doo·roon lyut·fehn*

Please fill out this form.

Burasını imzalayın lütfen. *boo·rah·sih·nih
eem·zah·lah·yihn lyut·fehn*

Please sign here.

(wireless) internet service	**(kablosuz) internet hizmeti** *(kahb·loh·sooz) een·tehr·neht heez·meh·tee*
room service	**oda servisi** *oh·dah sehr·vee·see*
a pool	**havuzu** *hah·voo·zoo*
a gym	**jimnastik** *jeem·nahs·teek*
I need...	**Bana bir...lâzım.** *bah·nah...liah·zihm*
an extra bed	**ek yatak** *ehk yah·tahk*
a cot	**bebek yatağı** *beh·behk yah·tah·gih*
a crib	**çocuk yatağı** *choh·jook yah·tah·gih*

For Numbers, see page 176.

Price

How much per night/week?	**Geceliği/Haftalığı ne kadar?** geh·jeh·lee·<u>yee</u>/hahf·tah·lih·<u>ih</u> neh kah·dahr
Does the price include breakfast/sales tax [VAT]?	**Fiyata kahvaltı/KDV dahil mi?** fee·yah·<u>tah</u> kah·vahl·<u>tih</u>/kah·deh·<u>veh</u> dah·<u>heel</u> mee

Preferences

Can I see the room?	**Odayı görebilir miyim?** oh·die·yih gur·reh·bee·leer mee·yeem
I'd like a…room.	**…bir oda istiyorum** …beer oh·dah ees·tee·yoh·room
better	**Daha iyi** dah·hah ee·yih
bigger	**Daha büyük** dah·hah byu·yuhk
cheaper	**Daha ucuz** dah·hah oo·jooz
quieter	**Daha sessiz** dah·hah sehs·seez
I'll take it.	**Alıyorum.** ah·lih·yoh·room
No, I won't take it.	**Almıyorum.** ahl·mih·yoh·room

Questions

Where's...?	**...nerede?** ..._neh_·reh·deh
the bar	**Bar** bahr
the bathrooms	**Tuvalet** too·vah·_leht_
the elevator [lift]	**Asansör** ah·sahn·_surr_
Can I have...?	**...alabilir miyim?** ...ah·lah·bee·_leer_ mee·yeem
a blanket	**Battaniye** baht·tah·nee·_yeh_
an iron	**Ütü** yu·_tyu_
a pillow	**Yastık** yahs·_tihk_
soap	**Sabun** sah·_boon_
toilet paper	**Tuvalet kağıdı** too·vah·_leht_ kah·ih·_dih_
a towel	**Havlu** hahv·_loo_
Do you have an adapte for this?	**Bunun için bir adaptörünüz var mı?** boo·_noon_ ee·cheen ah·dahp·tur·ryu·_nyuz_ _vahr_ mih
How do I turn on the lights?	**Işıkları nasıl açabilirim?** ih·shihk·lah·_rih_ _nah_·sihl ah·chah·bee·_lee_·reem
Could you wake me at...?	**Beni saat...oyandırabilir misiniz?** beh·_nee_ sah·_aht_...oh·yahn·dih·rah·bee·_leer_ mee·see·neez

YOU MAY SEE...

İTİNİZ/ÇEKİNİZ	push/pull
TUVALET	restroom [toilet]
DUŞ	shower
ASANSÖR	elevator [lift]
MERDİVENLER	stairs
ÇAMAŞIRHANE	laundry
RAHATSIZ ETMEYİNİZ	do not disturb
YANGIN KAPISI	fire door
ACİL ÇIKIŞ	emergency exit
ARAMA-UYANDIRMA	wake-up call

Turkish electricity is generally 220 volts, though 110 volts may be found in the European part of Istanbul. British and American appliances will need an adapter.

Can I leave this in the safe?	**Bunu kasada bırakabilir miyim?** *boo·noo kah·sah·dah bih·rah·kah·bee·leer mee·yeem?*
Could I have my things from the safe?	**Kasadan eşyalarımı alabilir miyim?** *kah·sah·<u>dahn</u> ehsh·<u>yah</u>·lah·rih·mih ah·lah·bee·<u>leer</u>·mee·yeem*
Is there mail/a message for me?	**Benim için posta/mesaj var mı?** *beh·<u>neem</u> ee·cheen pohs·<u>tah</u>/meh·<u>sahj</u> <u>vahr</u> mih*
Do you have a laundry service?	**Çamaşırhane hizmetiniz var mı?** *chah·mah·shihr·hah·neh heez·meh·tee·neez vahr mih*

For Time, see page 177.

Problems

There's a problem.	**Bir sorun var.** *beer soh·<u>roon</u> vahr*
I've lost my key/key card.	**Anahtarımı/Anahtar kartımı kaybettim.** *ah·nah·tah·rih·<u>mih</u>/ah·nah·<u>tahr</u> kahr·tih·<u>mih</u> <u>kie</u>·beht·teem*
I've locked myself out of my room.	**Kapıda kaldım.** *kah·pih·<u>dah</u> kahl·<u>dihm</u>*
There's no hot water/toilet paper.	**Sıcak su/Tuvalet kağıdı yok.** *sih·<u>jahk</u> soo/too·vah·<u>leht</u> kah·ih·<u>dih</u> yok*
The room is dirty.	**Oda kirli.** *oh·<u>dah</u> keer·<u>leeh</u>*
There are bugs in our room.	**Odamızda böcek var.** *oh·dah·mihz·<u>dah</u> bur·<u>jehk</u> vahr*

Can you fix…?	**…tamir edebilir misiniz?** … *tah·meer eh·deh·bee·leer·mee·see·neez*
the air conditioning	**Klimayı** *klee·mah·yih*
the fan	**Vantilatörü** *vahn·tee·lah·tur·ryu*
the heat [heating]	**Isıtıcıyı** *ih·sih·tih·jih·yih*
the light	**Işığı** *ih·shih·ih*
the TV	**Televizyonu** *teh·leh·vee·zyoh·noo*
the toilet	**Tuvaleti** *too·vah·leh·tee*
…has broken down.	**…kırık.** … *kih·rihk*
I'd like to move to another room.	**Başka bir odaya taşınmak istiyorum.** *bahsh·kah beer oh·dah·yah tah·shihn·mahk ees·tee·yoh·room*

Tipping in hotels is not necessary, but you may offer a few Lira
to porters or to attentive staff for their help.

Checking Out

When's check-out?	**Saat kaçta otelden ayrılmamız gerekiyor?** *sah•aht kahch•tah oh•tehl•dehn ie•rihl•mah•mihz geh•reh•kee•yohr*
Could I leave my bags here until…?	**Çantalarımı buraya…bırakabilir miyim?** *chan•tah•lah•rih•mih boo•rah•yah… bih•rah•kah•bee•leer mee•yeem*
Can I have an itemized bill/a receipt?	**Dökümlü hesap/Fiş alabilir miyim?** *dur•kyum•lyu heh•sahp/feesh ah•lah•bee•leer mee•yeem*
I think there's a mistake in this bill.	**Sanırım bu hesapta bir yanlışlık var.** *sah•nih•rihm boo heh•sahp•tah beer yan•lihsh•lihk vahr*
I'll pay in cash/by credit card.	**Nakit/Kredi kartı ile ödeyeceğim.** *nah•keet/ kreh•dee kahr•tih ee•leh ur•deh•yeh•jeh•yeem*

Renting

I've reserved an apartment/a room.	**Bir apartman/oda tuttum.** *beer ah•pahrt•mahn/ oh•dah toot•toom*
My name is…	**İsmim…** *ees•meem…*
Can I have the key/ key card?	**Anahtarı/Anahtar kartını alabilir miyim?** *ah•nah•tah•rih/ah•nah•tahr kahr•tih•nih ah•lah•bee•leer•mee•yeem*

Are there...?	**...var mı?** ... _vahr_ mih
dishes	**Tabak çanak** tah·_bahk_ chah·_nahk_
pillows	**Yastık** yahs·_tihk_
sheets	**Çarşaf** chahr·_shahf_
towels	**Havlu** hahv·_loo_
When/Where do I put out the bins?	**Çöpü ne zaman/nereye çıkarayım?** chur·_pyu_ neh zah·mahn/neh·reh·_yeh_ chih·kah·rah·yihm
...is broken.	**...bozuldu.** ... boh·zool·_doo_
How does...work?	**...nasıl çalışıyor?** ... _nah_·sihl chah·lih·_shih_·yohr
the air conditioner	**Klima** klee·_mah_
the dishwasher	**Bulaşık makinesi** boo·lah·_shihk_ mah·kee·neh·_see_
the freezer	**Dondurucu** dohn·doo·roo·_joo_
the heater	**Isıtıcı** ih·sih·tih·_jih_
the microwave	**Mikrodalga** meek·roh·dahl·_gah_
the refrigerator	**Buzdolabı** _booz_·doh·lah·_bih_
the stove	**Fırın** fih·_rihn_
the washing machine	**Çamaşır makinesi** chah·mah·_shihr_ mah·kee·neh·_see_

Domestic Items

I need...	**...ihtiyacım var.** ... eeh·tee·yah·_jihm_ vahr
an adapter	Adaptöre ah·dahp·tur·_reh_
aluminum [kitchen] foil	**Alimünyum kağıdına** ah·lee·_myu_·nyoom kah·ih·_dih_·nah
a bottle opener	**Şişe açacağına** shee·_sheh_ ah·chah·jah·ih·_nah_
a broom	**Süpürgeye** syu·pyur·geh·_yeh_
a can opener	**Konserve açacağına** kohn·_sehr_·veh ah·chah·jah·ih·_nah_
cleaning supplies	**Temizlik maddelerine** teh·meez·_leek_ mahd·deh·leh·ree·_neh_
a corkscrew	**Şarap açacağına** shah·_rahp_ ah·chah·jah·ih·_nah_

detergent	**Deterjana** deh·tehr·jah·<u>nah</u>	
dishwashing liquid	**Bulaşık deterjanına** boo·lah·<u>shihk</u> deh·tehr·jah·nih·<u>nah</u>	
garbage [rubbish] bags	**Çöp torbalarına** churp tohr·bah·lah·rih·<u>nah</u>	
a light bulb	**Ampula** ahm·poo·<u>lah</u>	
matches	**Kibrite** keeb·ree·<u>teh</u>	
a mop	**Yer bezine** yehr beh·zee·<u>neh</u>	
napkins	**Kağıt peçeteye** kah·<u>iht</u> peh·<u>cheh</u>·teh·yeh	
paper towels	**Kağıt havluya** kah·<u>iht</u> hahv·loo·<u>yah</u>	
plastic wrap [cling film]	**Plastik ambalaj** kah·ğı·dına plahs·<u>teek</u> ahm·bah·<u>lahj</u> kah·ih·dih·<u>nah</u>	
a plunger	**Plançere** <u>plahn</u>·cheh·reh	
scissors	**Makasa** mah·kah·<u>sah</u>	
a vacuum cleaner	**Elektrikli süpürgeye** eh·lehk·treek·<u>lee</u> syu·pyur·geh·<u>yeh</u>	

For In the Kitchen, see page 84.

For Oven Temperatures, see page 182.

At the Hostel

Do you have any places left for tonight?	**Bu gece için yer var mı?** boo geh·<u>jeh</u> ee·cheen yehr <u>vahr</u> mih

Hostels are located throughout Turkey and are a good option for those traveling through Turkey on a restricted budget. Keep in mind, though, that you usually need to be a card-holder in order to stay in a hostel here.

Can I have…?	**…alabilir miyim?** …ah·lah·bee·<u>leer</u> mee·yeem
a single/double room	**tek kişilik/çift kişilik oda** tehk kee·shee·leek/ cheeft kee·shee·leek oh·dah
a blanket	**Battaniye** baht·tah·nee·<u>yeh</u>
a pillow	**Yastık** yahs·<u>tihk</u>
sheets	**Çarşaf** chahr·<u>shahf</u>
towels	**Havlu** hahv·<u>loo</u>
What time do you lock up?	**Kapılar saat kaçta kapanıyor?** kah·pih·<u>lahr</u> sah·<u>aht</u> kahch·<u>tah</u> kah·pah·nih·yohr
Do I need a membership card?	**Üyelik kartına ihtiyacım var mı?** yu·yeh·leek kahr·tih·nah eeh·tee·yah·jihm vahr mih?
Here's my international student card.	**Buyrun uluslararası öğrenci kartım.** booy·roon oo·loos·lahr·ah·rah·sih ur·rehn·jee kahr·tihm

---

YOU MAY SEE…

İÇME SUYU	drinking water
KAMP YAPMAK YASAKTIR	no camping
ATEŞ/MANGAL YAKMAK YASAKTIR	no fires/barbecues

Going Camping

Can I camp here?	**Burada kamp yapabilir miyim?** _boo_·rah·dah kahmp yah·pah·bee·_leer_ mee·yeem
Is there a campsite near here?	**Yakınlarda bir kamp alanı var mı?** yah·_kihn_·lahr·_dah_ beer _kahmp_ ah·lah·nih _vahr_ mih
What is the charge per day/week?	**Günlüğü/Haftalığı ne kadar?** _gyun_·lyu·_yu_/ hahf·tah·lih·_ih_ _neh_ kah·dahr
Are there…?	**…var mı?** … _vahr_ mih
cooking facilities	**Pişirme olanakları** pee·sheer·_meh_ oh·lah·nahk·lah·_rih_
electric outlets	**Elektrik prizi** eh·lehk·_treek_ pree·_zee_
laundry facilities	**Çamaşırhane** chah·mah·_shihr_·hah·_neh_
showers	**Duş** doosh
tents for hire	**Kiralık çadırlar** kee·rah·_lihk_ chah·dihr·_lahr_
Where can I empty the chemical toilet?	**Portatif tuvaleti nereye dökebilirim?** pohr·tah·_teef_ too·vah·leh·_tee_ _neh_·reh·yeh dur·keh·bee·_lee_·reem

For Domestic Items, see page 49.

For In the Kitchen, see page 84.

Communications

ESSENTIAL

Where's an internet cafe?	**İnternet kafe nerede?** *een·tehr·neht kah·feh neh·reh·deh*
Can I access the internet/check e-mail here?	**Burada internete girebilir/postalarımı kontrol edebilir miyim?** *boo·rah·dah een·tehr·neh·teh gee·reh·bee·leer/pohs·tah·lah·rih·mih kohn·trohl eh·deh·bee·leer mee·yeem*
How much per hour/ half hour?	**Saati/Yarım saati ne kadar?** *sah·ah·tee/ yah·rihm sah·ah·tee neh kah·dahr*
How do I connect/ log on?	**Nasıl bağlanabilirim/girebilirim?** *nah·sihl bah·lah·nah·bee·lee·reem/gee·reh·bee·lee·reem*
I'd like a phone card, please.	**Bir telefon kartı lütfen.** *beer teh·leh·fohn kahr·tih lyut·fehn*
Can I have your phone number?	**Telefon numaranızı öğrenebilir miyim?** *teh·leh·fohn noo·mah·rah·nih·zih ur·reh·neh·bee·leer mee·yeem*
Here's my number/ e-mail address.	**İşte numaram/e-posta adresim.** *eesh·teh noo·mah·rahm/eh·pohs·tah ahd·reh·seem*
Call me.	**Beni arayın.** *beh·nee ah·rah·yihn*
E-mail me.	**Bana yazın.** *bah·nah yah·zihn*
Hello, this is…	**Merhaba, ben…** *mehr·hah·bah behn…*
I'd like to speak to…	**…ile konuşmak istiyorum.** *…ee·leh koh·noosh·mahk ees·tee·yoh·room*
Can you repeat that, please?	**Tekrar eder misiniz lütfen?** *tehk·rahr eh·dehr mee·see·neez lyut·fehn*
I'll call back later.	**Daha sonra arayacağım.** *dah·hah sohn·rah ah·rah·yah·jah·ihm*

Goodbye. (said by first person)	**Hoşçakalın.** hosh-_chah_ kah-lihn
Goodbye. (said by the other person)	**Güle güle.** gyu-_leh_ gyu-_leh_
Where is the post office?	**Postane nerede?** pohs-tah-_neh_ neh-reh-deh
I'd like to send this to...	**Bunu...göndermek istiyorum.** boo-_noo_... gurn-dehr-_mehk_ ees-_tee_-yoh-room

Online

Where's an internet cafe?	**İnternet kafe nerede?** een-tehr-_neht_ kah-_feh_ _neh_-reh-deh
Does it have wireless internet?	**Kablosuz internet var mı?** kahb-loh-_sooz_ een-tehr-_neht_ _vahr_ mih
What is the WiFi password?	**Kablosuz ağın şifresi nedir?** kahb-loh-sooz ah-ihn sheef-reh-see neh-deer
Is the WiFi free?	**Kablosuz ağ ücretsiz mi?** kahb-loh-sooz ah yuch-reht-seez-mee
Do you have bluetooth?	**Bluetooth var mı?** Bluetooth vahr mih
How do I turn the computer on/off?	**Bilgisayarı nasıl açabilirim/kapatabilirim?** beel-gee-sah-yah-_rih_ _nah_-sihl ah-chah-bee-_lee_-reem/ kah-pah-tah-bee-_lee_-reem
Can I...?	**...bilir miyim?** ...bee-_leer_ mee-yeem
access the internet here	**Buradan internete bağlana** _boo_-rah-dahn een-tehr-neh-_teh_ bah-lah-nah
check e-mail	**E-postaya baka** eh-poh-stah-_yah_ bah-_kah_
print	**Basa** bah-_sah_
plug in/charge my laptop/iPhone/iPad/	**diz üstü bilgisayarımı/iPhone'umu/iPad'imi fişe takabilir miyim/şarj edebilir miyim?**

BlackBerry?	*Deez yus•tyu beel•gee•sah•yah•rih•mi/iPhone'um•hu/ iPad'im•hi feesh•eh tah•kah•bee•leer mee•yeem/sharj eh•deh•bee•leer mee•yeem*
access Skype?	**Skype'ı kullanabilir miyim?** *Skype'ih kool•lah•nah•bee•leer mee•yeem*
How much per hour/ half hour?	**Saati/Yarım saati ne kadar?** *sah•ah•<u>tee</u>/yah•<u>rihm</u> sah•ah•<u>tee</u> neh kah•dahr*
How do I…?	**Nasıl…?** *<u>nah</u>•sihl…*
connect/disconnect	**bağlanırım/bağlantıyı keserim** *bagh•lah•nih• rihm/bah•lahn•tih•<u>yih</u> keh•<u>seh</u>•reem*
log on/off	**giriş/çıkış yaparım** *gee•<u>reesh</u>/chih•<u>kihsh</u> yah•<u>pah</u>•rihm*
type this symbol	**bu sembolü yazarım** *<u>boo</u> sehm•boh•<u>lyu</u> yah•<u>zah</u>•rehm*
What's your e-mail?	**E-posta adresiniz nedir?** *eh•pohs•<u>tah</u> ahd•reh•see•<u>neez</u> <u>neh</u>•deer*
My e-mail is…	**E-posta adresim…** *eh•pohs•<u>tah</u> ahd•reh•<u>seem</u>…*

Social Media

Are you on Facebook/ Twitter?	**Facebook/Twitter'da mısın?** *Facebook/Twitter'dah mih•sihn*
What's your user name?	**Kullanıcı adın ne?** *kool•lah•nih•jih ah•dihn neh*

I'll add you as a friend.	**Seni arkadaş olarak ekleyeceğim.** *seh·nee ahr·kah·dash oh·lah·rahk ehk·leh·yeh·jeh·yeem*
I'll follow you on Twitter.	**Seni Twitter'da takip edeceğim.** *seh·nee Twitter'dah tah·keep eh·deh·jeh·yeem*
Are you following...?	**... takip ediyor musun?** *... tah·keep eh·dee yohr moo soon*
I'll put the pictures on Facebook/Twitter.	**Resimleri Facebook/Twitter'a koyacağım.** *reh·seem·leh·ree Facebook/Tweeter'ah koh·yah·jah·yihm*
I'll tag you in the pictures.	**Seni resimlerde etiketleyeceğim.** *seh·nee reh·seem·lehr·deh eh·tee·keht·lih·yeh·jeh·yeem*

Phone

A phone card/prepaid phone, please.	**Bir telefon kartı/kontörlü telefon lütfen.** *beer teh·leh·_fohn_ kahr·_tih_/kohn·tyur·_lyu_ teh·leh·_fohn_ _lyut_·fehn*
How much?	**Ne kadar?** *neh kah·dahr*
My phone doesn't work here.	**Telefonum burda çalışmıyor.** *teh·leh·foh·_noom_ boor·_dah_ chah·_lihsh_·mih·yohr*
What's the area/country code for...?	**...için bölge/ülke kodu nedir?** *... ee·_cheen_ burl·_geh_/yul·_keh_ koh·_doo_ neh·deer*

YOU MAY SEE...

KAPAT	close
SİL	delete
E-POSTA	e-mail
ÇIKIŞ	logout
YARDIM	help
ANINDA MUHABBET	instant messenger
İNTERNET	internet
GİRİŞ	login
YENI MESAJ	new message
AÇ/KAPA	on/off
AÇİK	open
YAZDIR	print
KAYDET	save
GÖNDER	send
KULLANICI İSMİ/ŞİFRE	username/password
KABLOSUZ İNTERNET	wireless internet

What's the number for Information?	**Bilinmeyen numaralar kaç?** bee•<u>leen</u>•meh•yehn noo•<u>mah</u>•rah•lahr <u>kahch</u>
I'd like the number for…	**…için numarayı istiyorum.** …ee•<u>cheen</u> noo•<u>mah</u>•rah•yih ees•<u>tee</u>•yoh•room
Can I have your number?	**Telefon numaranızı öğrenebilir miyim?** teh•leh•<u>fohn</u> noo•<u>mah</u>•rah•nih•zih ur•reh•neh•bee•<u>leer</u> mee•yeem
Here's my number.	**İşte numaram.** eesh•<u>teh</u> noo•<u>mah</u>•rahm

Please call me. **Lütfen beni arayın.** _lyut_•fehn beh•_nee_ ah•_rah_•yihn

Please text me. **Lütfen bana yazın.** _lyut_•fehn bah•_nah yah_•zihn

I'll call you. **Sizi arayacağım.** see•_zee_ ah•rah•yah•_jah_•yihm

I'll text you. **Size yazarım.** see•_zeh_ yah•_zah_•rihm

For Numbers, see page 176.

YOU MAY HEAR...

Kim arıyor? _keem_ ah•_rih_•yohr — Who's calling?

Bir dakika lütfen. — Hold on, please.
beer dah•kee•_kah lyut_•fehn

Telefona gelemez. _teh_•leh•foh•_nah_ — He/She can't come to the
geh•_leh_•mehz — phone.

Mesaj bırakmak istiyor musunuz? — Would you like to leave a
meh•_sahj_ bih•rahk•_mahk_ ees•_tee_•yohr — message?
moo•_soo_•nooz

Daha sonra/On dakika içinde arayın. — Call back later/in 10
dah•_hah_ _sohn_•rah/ohn dah•kee•_kah_ ee•cheen• — minutes.
deh ah•_rah_•yihn

Sizi tekrar arayabilir mi? see•_zee_ tehk•_rahr_ — Can he/she call you
back?
ah•rah•yah•bee•_leer_ mee

Telefon numaranızı öğrenebilir miyim? — What's your number?
teh•leh•_fohn_ noo•_mah_•rah•nih•zih
ur•reh•neh•bee•_leer_ mee•yeem

Telephone Etiquette

Hello, this is…	**Merhaba, ben…** _mehr•hah•bah behn_…
I'd like to speak to…	**…ile konuşmak istiyorum.** …_ee•leh koh•noosh•mahk ees•tee•yoh•room_
Extension…	**Dahili hattı…** _dah•hee•lee haht•tih_…
Can you speak louder/ more slowly, please?	**Daha yüksek/yavaş sesle konuşur musunuz lütfen?** _dah•hah yuk•sehk/yah•vahsh sehs•leh koh•noo•shoor moo•soo•nooz lyut•fehn_
Can you repeat that, please?	**Tekrar eder misiniz lütfen?** _tehk•rahr eh•dehr mee•see•neez lyut•fehn_
I'll call back later.	**Daha sonra tekrar ararım.** _dah•hah sohn•rah tehk•rahr ah•rah•rihm_
Goodbye. (said by first person)	**Hoşçakalın.** _hosh•chah kah•lihn_
Goodbye. (said by second person)	**Güle güle.** _gyu•leh gyu•leh_

For Business Travel, see page 147.

YOU MAY HEAR...

Lütfen gümrük beyanını doldurunuz.
*lyut•fehn gyum•ryuk beh•yah•nih•nih
dohl•doo•roo•nooz*

Değeri nedir? *deh•yeh•ree neh•deer*

İçinde ne var? *ee•cheen•deh neh vahr*

Please fill out the customs
declaration form.

What's the value?

What's inside?

Fax

Can I send/receive a fax here?	**Buradan faks gönderebilir/alabilir miyim?** *boo•rah•dahn fahks gurn•deh•reh•bee•leer/ ah•lah•bee•leer mee•yeem*
What's the fax number?	**Faks numarası kaç?** *fahks noo•mah•rah•sih kahch*
Please fax this to...	**Lütfen bunu...fakslayın.** *lyut•fehn boo•noo... fahks•lah•yihn*

Post

Where's the post office/ mailbox [postbox]?	**Postahane/Posta kutusu nerede?** *pohs·tah·neh/ pohs·tah koo·too·soo neh·reh·deh*
A stamp for this postcard/letter, please.	**Bu kartpostal/mektup için pul lütfen.** *boo kahrt·pohs·tahl/mehk·toop ee·cheen pool lyut·fehn*
How much?	**Ne kadar?** *neh kah·dahr*
I want to send this package by airmail/ express.	**Bu paketi uçak/özel ulak ile göndermek istiyorum.** *boo pah·keh·tee oo·chahk/ur·zehl oo·lahk ee·leh gurn·dehr·mehk ees·tee·yoh·room*
A receipt, please.	**Lütfen bir fiş verin.** *lyut·fehn beer feesh veh·reen*

Post offices in Turkey display a yellow sign with the letters **PTT (Posta Telegraf Telefon)** (Post Telegraph Telephone) in blue. Aside from sending letters or packages, you can also change money, make phone calls or buy phone cards. Major post offices in more touristy areas may stay open until midnight, with a more restricted schedule on Sunday. Smaller post offices are generally only open until 5:00 p.m.

Food & Drink

ESSENTIAL

Can you recommend a good restaurant/bar?	**İyi bir lokanta/bar önerebilir misiniz?** *ee•yee beer loh•kahn•tah/bahr ur•neh•reh•bee•leer mee•see•neez*
Is there a traditional Turkish/an inexpensive restaurant near here?	**Yakınlarda geleneksel Türk yemekleri/ucuz yemek sunan bir lokanta var mı?** *yah•kihn•lahr•dah geh•leh•nehk•sehl tyurk yeh•mehk•leh•ree/oo•jooz yeh•mehk soo•nahn beer loh•kahn•tah vahr mih*
A table for..., please.	**...kişi için bir masa lütfen.** *...kee•shee ee•cheen beer mah•sah lyut•fehn*
Could we sit...?	**...oturabilir miyiz?** *...oh•too•rah•bee•leer mee•yeez*
here/there	**Burada/Orada** *boo•rah•dah/oh•rah•dah*
outside	**Dışarda** *dih•shah•rih•dah*
in a non-smoking area	**Sigara içilmeyen bir yerde** *see•gah•rah ee•cheel•meh•yehn beer yehr•deh*
I'm waiting for someone.	**Birini bekliyorum.** *bee•ree•nee behk•lee•yoh•room*
Where are the restrooms [toilets]?	**Tuvalet nerede?** *too•vah•leht neh•reh•deh*
A menu, please.	**Menü lütfen.** *meh•nyu lyut•fehn*
What do you recommend?	**Ne önerirsiniz?** *neh ur•neh•reer•see•neez*
I'd like...	**...istiyorum.** *...ees•tee•yoh•room*
Some more..., please.	**Biraz daha...istiyorum lütfen.** *bee•rahz dah•hah...ees•tee•yoh•room lyut•fehn*

Enjoy your meal.	**Afiyet olsun.**	*ah·fee·yeht ohl·soon*
The check [bill], please.	**Hesap lütfen.**	*heh·sahp lyut·fehn*
Is service included?	**Servis dahil mi?**	*sehr·vees dah·heel mee*
Can I pay by credit card?	**Kredi kartı ile ödeme yapabilir miyim?**	*kreh·dee kahr·tih ee·leh ur·deh·meh yah·pah·bee·leer mee·yeem*
Can I have a receipt please?	**Lütfen fiş alabilir miyim?**	*lyut·fehn feesh ah·lah·bee·leer mee·yeem*
Thank you.	**Teşekkür ederim.**	*teh·shehk·kyur eh·deh·reem*

Where to Eat

Can you recommend...?	**...önerebilir misiniz?**	*...ur·neh·reh·bee·leer mee·see·neez*
a restaurant	**Lokanta**	*loh·kahn·tah*
a bar	**Bar**	*bahr*
a cafe	**Kafe**	*kah·feh*
a fast-food place	**Hazır yemek lokantası**	*hah·zihr yeh·mehk loh·kahn·tah·sih*
a cheap restaurant	**ucuz bir restoran**	*oo jooz beer res·toh·rahn*
an expensive restaurant	**pahalı bir restoran**	*pah·hah·lih beer res·toh·rahn*
a restaurant with a good view	**güzel manzaralı bir restoran**	*gyu·zehl mahn·zah·rah·lih beer res·toh·rahn*
an authentic/ a non-touristy restaurant	**otantik turistik olmayan bir restoran**	*oh·tahn·teek/too·rist·eek ohl·mah·yahn beer res·toh·rahn*

Reservations & Preferences

I'd like to reserve a table…	**…bir masa ayırtmak istiyorum.** *…beer mah·<u>sah</u> ah·yihrt·<u>mahk</u> ees·<u>tee</u>·yoh·room*
for two	**İki kişi için** *ee·<u>kee</u> kee·<u>shee</u> ee·cheen*
for this evening	**Bu gece** *boo geh·jeh*
for tomorrow at…	**Yarın saat…için** *yah·<u>rihn</u> sah·<u>aht</u>…ee·cheen*
A table for two, please.	**İki kişilik bir masa lütfen.** *ee·<u>kee</u> kee·shee·<u>leek</u> beer mah·<u>sah</u> <u>lyut</u>·fehn*
We have a reservation.	**Yer ayırtmıştık.** *yehr ah·yihrt·<u>mihsh</u>·tihk*
My name is…	**İsmim…** *ees·<u>meem</u>…*
Could we sit…?	**…oturabilir miyiz?** *…oh·too·rah·bee·<u>leer</u> mee·yeez*
here/there	**Burada/Orada** *boo·rah·dah/<u>oh</u>·rah·dah*
outside	**Dışarda** *dih·<u>shahr</u>·dah*
in a non-smoking area	**Sigara içilmeyen bir yerde** *see·gah·<u>rah</u> ee·<u>cheel</u>·meh·yehn beer yehr·<u>deh</u>*
by the window	**Pencere kenarında** *pehn·jeh·<u>reh</u> keh·nah·rihn·<u>dah</u>*
Where are the toilets?	**Tuvalet nerede?** *too·vah·<u>leht</u> <u>neh</u>·reh·deh*

Can I get a table in the shade/sun? **Gölgede/güneşte bir masa alabilir miyim?**
gurl•geh•deh/gyu•nash•teh beer mah•sah ah•lah•bee•leer mee•yeem

For Time, see page 177.

YOU MAY HEAR...

Rezervasyonunuz var mı?
reh•zehr•vah•syoh•noo•nooz vahr mih
Ne kadar? _neh kah•dahr_
Sigara içilen bölümde mi içilmeyen bölümde mi? _see•gah•rah ee•chee•lehn bur•lyum•deh mee ee•cheel•meh•yehn bur•lyum•deh mee_
Siparişinizi vermeye hazır mısınız?
see•pah•ree•shee•nee•zee vehr•meh•yeh hah•zihr mih•sih•nihz
Ne istersiniz? _neh ees•tehr•see•neez_
...öneririm. . . .ur•neh•ree•reem
Afiyet olsun. _ah•fee•yeht ohl•soon_

Do you have a reservation?

How many?

Smoking or non-smoking?

Are you ready to order?

What would you like?
I recommend...
Enjoy your meal.

How to Order

Waiter!/Waitress!	**Garson!** *gahr•sohn*	
We're ready to order.	**Siparişleri verebiliriz.** *see•pah•reesh•leh•ree veh•reh•bee•lee•reez*	
May I see the wine list, please?	**Şarap listesini görebilir miyim lütfen?** *shah•rahp lees•teh•see•nee gur•reh•bee•leer mee•yeem lyut•fehn*	
I'd like...	**...istiyorum.** *...ees•tee•yoh•room*	
a bottle of...	**Bir şişe...** *beer shee•sheh...*	
a carafe of...	**Bir sürahi...** *beer syu•rah•hee...*	
a glass of...	**Bir bardak...** *beer bahr•dahk...*	
The menu, please.	**Menü lütfen.** *meh•nyu lyut•fehn*	
Do you have...?	**...var mı?** *...vahr mih*	
a menu in English	**İngilizce menü** *een•gee•leez•jeh meh•nyu*	
a fixed-price menu	**Fiks menü** *feeks meh•nyu*	
a children's menu	**Çocuk menüsü** *choh•jook meh•nyu•syu lyut•fehn*	
What do you recommend?	**Ne önerirsiniz?** *neh ur•neh•reer•see•neez*	
What's this?	**Bu nedir?** *boo neh•deer*	
What's in it?	**İçinde ne var?** *ee•cheen•deh neh vahr*	
Is it spicy?	**Baharatlı mı?** *bah•hah•raht•lih mih*	
It's to go [take away].	**Paket olacak.** *pah•keht oh•lah•jahk*	
I'd like...	**...istiyorum.** *...ees•tee•yoh•room*	
More..., please.	**Daha...lütfen.** *dah•hah... lyut•fehn*	
With/Without...	**...ile/-siz.** *...ee•leh/•seez*	
I can't have...	**...yiyemem.** *...yee•yeh•mehm*	
I'd like...	**...istiyorum.** *...ees•tee•yoh•room*	
More..., please.	**Daha...lütfen.** *dah•hah... lyut•fehn*	
With/Without...	**...ile/-siz.** *...ee•leh/•seez*	
I can't have...	**...yiyemem.** *...yee•yeh•mehm*	
I'd like...	**...istiyorum.** *...ees•tee•yoh•room*	
More..., please.	**Daha...lütfen.** *dah•hah... lyut•fehn*	

With/Without…	**…ile/-siz**. … _ee_•leh/•seez
I can't have…	**…yiyemem**. … yee•_yeh_•mehm
rare	**az pişmiş** _ahz_ peesh•meesh
medium	**orta ateşte** ohr•_tah_ ah•tehsh•_teh_
well-done	**iyi pişmiş** ee•_yee_ peesh•meesh

YOU MAY SEE…

MASA ÜCRETİ	cover charge
FİKS MENÜ	fixed-price
MENÜ	menu
GÜNÜN MENÜSÜ	menu of the day
HİZMET DAHİL (DEĞİL)	service (not) included
SPESİYALLER	specials

Cooking Methods

baked	**fırında pişmiş**	fih·rihn·<u>dah</u> peesh·meesh
boiled	**haşlanmış**	hash·lahn·<u>mihsh</u>
braised	**hafif ateşte pişmiş**	hah·<u>feef</u> ah·<u>tesh</u>·teh peesh·meesh
breaded	**ekmek kırıntıları ile kızartılmış**	ehk·<u>mehk</u> kih·rihn·tih·lah·<u>rih</u> ee·leh kih·<u>zahr</u>·tihl·mihsh
creamed	**kremalı**	kreh·mah·<u>lih</u>
diced	**kuşbaşı doğranmış**	<u>koosh</u>·bah·shih doh·rahn·<u>mihsh</u>
filleted	**filetolanmış**	fee·<u>leh</u>·toh·lahn·mihsh
fried	**kızartma**	kih·zahrt·<u>mah</u>
grilled	**ızgara**	ihz·gah·<u>rah</u>
poached	**haşlama**	hahsh·lah·<u>mah</u>
roasted	**kızarmış**	kih·zahr·<u>mihsh</u>
sautéed	**sote**	soh·<u>teh</u>
smoked	**tütsülenmiş**	tyut·syu·lehn·<u>meesh</u>
steamed	**buğulama**	boo·oo·lah·<u>mah</u>
stewed	**yahni**	yah·<u>hnee</u>
stuffed	**dolma**	dohl·<u>mah</u>

69

Dietary Requirements

I'm...	**Ben...**	behn...
diabetic	**şeker hastasıyım**	sheh·<u>kehr</u> hahs·tah·<u>sih</u>·yihm
lactose intolerant	**laktoza duyarlıyım**	lahk·toh·<u>zah</u> doo·yahr·<u>lih</u>·yihm
vegetarian	**vejetaryenim**	veh·jeh·tahr·<u>yeh</u>·neem
vegan	**vejeteryan**	veh·zheh·tehr·yahn
I'm allergic to...	**...ya alerjim var.**	...yah ahl·lehr·<u>jeem</u> vahr
I can't eat...	**...içeren yiyecek yiyemem.**	...ee·cheh·<u>rehn</u> yee·yeh·<u>jehk</u> yee·<u>yeh</u>·mehm
dairy	**Süt ürünleri**	<u>syut</u> yu·ryun·leh·ree
gluten	**Glüten**	glyu·tehn

nuts	**Kuruyemiş** *koo·roo·yeh·meesh*
pork	**Domuz eti** *doh·mooz eh·tee*
shellfish	**Kabuklu deniz ürünleri** *kah·book·loo deh·neez yu·ryun·leh·ree*
spicy foods	**Baharatlı yiyecekler** *bah·hah·raht·lih yee·yeh·jehk·lehr*
wheat	**Hamur işleri** *hah·moor eesh·leh·ree*
Is it halal/kosher?	**Helal/Kaşer mi?** *heh·lahl/kah·shehr mee*
Do you have...?	**...var mı?** *... vahr mih*
skimmed milk	**yağsız süt** *yah·sihz syut*
whole milk	**tam yağlı süt** *tahm yah·lih syut*
soya milk	**soya sütü** *soh·yah syu·tyu*

Dining with Children

Do you have children's portions?	**Çocuk porsiyonunuz var mı?** *choh·jook pohr·see·yoh·noo·nooz vahr mih*
A highchair/child's seat, please.	**Yüksek sandalye/Çocuk sandalyesi lütfen.** *yuk·sehk sahn·dahl·yeh/choh·jook sahn·dahl·yeh·see lyut·fehn*
Where can I feed/ change the baby?	**Bebeği nerede besleyebilirim/üstünü değiştirebilirim?** *beh·beh·yee neh·reh·deh behs·leh·yeh·bee·lee·reem/yus·tyu·nyu deh·yeesh·tee·reh·bee·lee·reem*
Can you warm this?	**Bunu ısıtabilir misiniz?** *boo·noo ih·sih·tah·bee·leer mee·see·neez*

For Traveling with Children, see page 150.

How to Complain

How much longer will our food be?	**Yemek için daha ne kadar bekleyeceğiz?** *yeh·mehk ee·cheen dah·hah neh kah·dahr behk·leh·yeh·jeh·yeez*
We can't wait any longer.	**Daha fazla bekleyemeyeceğiz.** *dah·hah fahz·lah behk·leh·yeh·meh·yeh·jeh·yeez*
We're leaving.	**Gidiyoruz.** *gee·dee·yoh·rooz*
This isn't clean/fresh.	**Bu temiz/taze değil.** *boo teh·meez/ tah·zeh deh·yeel*
I can't eat this.	**Bunu yiyemem.** *boo·noo yee·yeh·mehm*
This is too…	**Bu çok…** *boo chohk…*
cold/hot	**soğuk/sıcak** *soh·ook/sih·jahk*
salty/spicy	**tuzlu/baharatlı** *tooz·loo/bah·hah·raht·lih*
tough/bland	**sert/yumuşak** *sehrt/yoo·moo·shahk*
I didn't order this.	**Benim siparişim bu değil.** *beh·neem see·pah·ree·sheem boo deh·yeel*
I ordered…	**…söyledim.** *…sur·yleh·deem*

Paying

The check [bill], please.	**Hesap lütfen.** *heh·sahp lyut·fehn*
We'd like to pay separately.	**Ayrı ayrı ödemek istiyoruz.** *ie·rih ie·rih ur·deh·mehk ees·tee·yoh·rooz*
It's all together.	**Hepsi birlikte lütfen.** *hehp·see beer·leek·teh lyut·fehn*
Is service included?	**Servis dahil mi?** *sehr·vees dah·heel mee*
What's this amount for?	**Bu miktar ne için?** *boo meek·tahr neh ee·cheen*
	Bunu almadım. ...aldım. *boo·noo ahl·mah·dihm. . .ahl·dihm*
	Kredi kartı ile ödeme yapabilir miyim? *kreh·dee kahr·tih ee·leh ur·deh·meh yah·pah·bee·leer mee·yeem*
	Dökümlü hesap/Fiş alabilir miyim? *dur·kyum·lyu heh·sahp/feesh ah·lah·bee·leer mee·yeem*
	Yemek çok güzeldi. *yeh·mehk chohk gyu·zehl·dee*
	Zaten ödedim. *zah·tehn ur·deh·deem*

Service is included in the price at cafes and restaurants. However, people do tend to leave a small tip. Round up the bill to the nearest euro or two for good service.

Meals & Cooking

Breakfast

bal *bahl*	honey
ekmek *ehk·mehk*	bread
greyfurt *gray·foort*	grapefruit
küçük yuvarlak ekmek *kyu·chyuk yoo·vahr·lahk ehk·mehk*	rolls
kızarmış ekmek *kih·zahr·mihsh ehk·mehk*	roasted bread
marmelat *mahr·meh·laht*	marmalade
meyve suyu *may·veh soo·yoo*	fruit juice
portakal *pohr·tah·kahl*	orange
reçel *reh·chehl*	jam
süt *syut*	milk
tereyağı *teh·reh·yah·ih*	butter
...yumurta *...yoo·moor·tah*	...eggs
çırpma *chihrp·mah*	scrambled
katı *kah·tih*	boiled
sahanda *sah·hahn·dah*	fried

Meze (appetizers) are the perfect accompaniment to a leisurely drink before dinner. **Meze** may be hot, **sıcak mezeler** (hot appetizers), or cold, **soğuk mezeler** (cold appetizers). The selection that is served usually depends on the main course to follow. Dried or marinated mackerel, vegetables cooked in oil, tomato and cucumber salad or deep fried mussels and calamari in sauce may precede grilled fish or meat. Hummus, marinated stuffed eggplant, lentil balls or spicy peppers with nuts might be served before a main dish of kebab.

Appetizers

arnavut ciğeri *ahr·nah·voot jee·yeh·ree*	fried liver morsels
beyaz peynir *beh·yahz pay·neer*	white cheese
börek *bur·rehk*	hot filo pastries
dolma *dohl·mah*	stuffed grape leaves
imam bayıldı *ee·mahm bah·yihl·dih*	stuffed eggplant [aubergine]
patlıcan salatası *paht·lih·jahn sah·lah·tah·sih*	eggplant [aubergine] salad
pilaki *pee·lah·kee*	beans in olive oil
tarama *tah·rah·mah*	fish roe pâté

Soup

balık çorbası *bah·lihk chohr·bah·sih*	fish soup
et suyuna çorba *eht soo·yoo·nah chohr·bah*	consommé
kremalı çorba *kreh·mah·lih chohr·bah*	cream soup
patates çorbası *pah·tah·tehs chohr·bah·sih*	potato soup
sebze çorbası *sehb·zeh chohr·bah·sih*	vegetable soup
soğan çorbası *soh·ahn chohr·bah·sih*	onion soup
tavuk çorbası *tah·vook chohr·bah·sih*	chicken soup

Fish & Seafood

ahtapot *ah·tah·poht*	octopus
alabalık *ah·lah·bah·lihk*	trout
deniz tarağı *deh·neez tah·rah·ih*	clams
ıstakoz *ihs·tah·kohz*	lobster
istiridye *ees·tee·reed·yeh*	oysters
kalamar *kah·lah·mahr*	squid
karides *kah·ree·dehs*	shrimp [prawns]
lüfer *lyu·fehr*	bluefish
midye *meed·yeh*	mussels
morina balığı *moh·ree·nah bah·lih·ih*	cod
pisi balığı *pee·see bah·lih·ih*	plaice

ringa balığı *reen·gah bah·lih·ih*   herring [whitebait]

ton balığı *tohn bah·lih·ih*   tuna

kılıç şiş *kih·lihch sheesh*   swordfish kebabs grilled with bay leaves, tomatoes and green peppers

Çınarcık usulü balık *chih·nahr·jihk oo·soo·lyu bah·lihk*   fried swordfish, sea bass and shrimp, served with mushrooms

uskumru pilakisi *oos·koom·roo pee·lah·kee·see*   mackerel fried in olive oil, with potatoes, celery, carrots and garlic; served cold

Meat & Poultry

bonfile *bohn·fee·leh*   steak

böbrek *bur·brehk*   kidneys

but *boot*   leg

but eti *boot eh·tee*   rump

ciğer *jee·ehr*   liver

Çerkez tavuğu *chehr·kehz tah·voo·oo*   Circassian chicken: boiled chicken with rice and nut sauce

çiğ köfte *chee kurf•teh* — raw meatballs made from ground meat and cracked wheat

dana *dah•nah* — veal

domuz *doh•mooz* — pork

dana pirzolası *dah•nah peer•zoh•lah•sih* — T-bone steak

fileto *fee•leh•toh* — fillet

hindi *heen•dee* — turkey

jambon *jahm•bohn* — ham

kemikli et *keh•meek•lee eht* — cutlet

kuzu *koo•zoo* — lamb

kuzu dolması *koo•zoo dohl•mah•sih* — lamb stuffed with savory rice, liver and pistachios

kuzu güveç *koo•zoo gyu•vehch* — lamb stew with onions, garlic, potatoes, tomatoes and herbs

ördek *ur•rdehk* — duck

pirzola *peer•zoh•lah* — chops

sığır eti *sih•ihr eh•tee* — beef

sığır filetosu *sih•ihr fee•leh•toh•soo* — sirloin

sosis *soh•sees* — sausages

sülün *syu•lyun* — pheasant

şiş köfte *sheesh kurf•teh* — ground lamb croquettes on a skewer, grilled over charcoal

tavuk *tah•vook* — chicken

tavşan *tahv•shahn* — rabbit

yoğurtlu kebab *yoh•oort•loo keh•bahb* — kebab on toasted bread with pureed tomatoes and seasoned yogurt

Turkish cuisine is complex, reflecting Turkey's situation as a crossroads where East meets West. You'll find there is a healthy emphasis on fresh meat, fish and vegetables mixed with spices. **Şiş kebab** (skewered cubes of meat) and **baklava** (filo pastry stuffed with honey and pistachio nuts) are two typical Turkish dishes known and enjoyed around the world.

Vegetables & Staples

bezelye *beh·zehl·yeh*	peas
biber *bee·behr*	peppers
domates *doh·mah·tehs*	tomatoes
havuç *hah·vooch*	carrots
hıyar *hih·yahr*	cucumber
kabak *kah·bahk*	zucchini [courgette]
kereviz *keh·reh·veez*	celery
lahana *lah·hah·nah*	cabbage
mantar *mahn·tahr*	mushrooms
marul *mah·rool*	lettuce
patates *pah·tah·tehs*	potatoes
patlıcan *paht·lih·jahn*	eggplant [aubergine]
pirinç *pee·reench*	rice
sarı şalgam *sah·rih shahl·gahm*	rutabaga [swede]
sarmısak *sahr·mih·sahk*	garlic
soğan *soh·ahn*	onions
şalgam *shahl·gahm*	turnips
taze fasulye *tah·zeh fah·sool·yeh*	green beans
taze soğan *tah·zeh soh·ahn*	shallots [spring onions]
dere otu *deh·reh oh·too*	dill

karanfil *kah·rahn·feel*   cloves
kekik *keh·keek*   thyme
kırmızı biber *kihr·mih·zih bee·behr*   chili
kimyon *keem·yohn*   cumin
kişniş *keesh·neesh*   cilantro
maydanoz *mie·dah·nohz*   parsley
nane *nah·neh*   mint
safran *sahf·rahn*   saffron

Dolma is the term for any stuffed vegetable. Stuffing may be made of a mix of ground meat, cheese, onion and tomato or may be a vegetarian rice stuffing with tomato, onion and garlic. Meat-filled **dolma** are usually served as a main course dish with yogurt sauce, while rice-filled **dolma** are usually cooked in olive oil and eaten at room temperature.

Fruit

ahududu *ah·hoo·doo·doo*	raspberries
çilek *chee·lehk*	strawberries
elma *ehl·mah*	apples
erik *eh·reek*	plums
greyfurt *gray·foort*	grapefruit
karpuz *kahr·pooz*	watermelon
kavun *kah·voon*	melon
kiraz *kee·rahz*	cherries
muz *mooz*	bananas
nar *nahr*	pomegranates
portakal *pohr·tah·kahl*	oranges
şeftali *shehf·tah·lee*	peaches
üzüm *yu·zyum*	grapes

Cheese

beyaz peynir *beh·yahz pay·neer*	white cheese
kaşar *kah·shahr*	hard cheese
otlu peynir *oht·loo pay·neer*	herb cheese
tulum peyniri *too·loom pay·nee·ree*	goat cheese

Dessert

aşure *ah·shoo·reh*	sweet, cold soup made of mixed grains, beans and dried fruits
ayva tatlısı *ie·vah taht·lih·sih*	baked quince slices in a syrup
baklava *bahk·lah·vah*	filo pastry filled with honey and pistachio nuts
kabak tatlısı *kah·bahk taht·lih·sih*	baked pumpkin in a syrup
kadayıf *kah·dah·yihf*	shredded wheat dessert, similar to baklava
kazandibi *kah·zahn·dee·bee*	oven-browned milk pudding
muhallebi *moo·hahl·leh·bee*	milk pudding
sütlaç *syut·lahch*	rice pudding
tavuk göğsü *tah·vook gur·hsyu*	milk pudding with thin filaments of chicken breast

The most common dessert after a meal is fresh seasonal fruit, though Turkish cooking offers a whole range of delights to try. Puddings, known as **muhallebi**, may or may not be milk-based and may be mixed with a variety of ingredients such as citrus fruit or even very thin slices of chicken breast. **Lokma** (dessert of fried dough dipped in syrup) and **helva** (sauteed flour and pine nuts mixed with milk and sugar or water) are also traditional desserts. The internationally-famous **baklava** (filo pastry stuffed with honey and pistachio nuts) is commonly eaten with coffee or after a kebab dish and the also well-known **lokum** (Turkish delight) is eaten as a digestive after meals.

Sauces & Condiments

salt	**tuz** *tooz*
pepper	**karabiber** *kah·rah·bee·behr*
mustard	**hardal** *hahr·dahl*
ketchup	**ketçap** *keht·chahp*

At the Market

Where are the carts [trolleys]/baskets?	**El arabaları/Sepetler nerede?** *ehl ah·rah·bah·lah·rih/seh·peht·lehr neh·reh·deh*
Where is…?	**…nerede?** *…neh·reh·deh*
I'd like some of that/those.	**Şundan/Şunlardan biraz istiyorum.** *shoon·dahn/shoon·lahr·dahn beer·ahz ees·tee·yoh·room*
Can I taste it?	**Tadına bakabilir miyim?** *tah·dih·nah bah·kah·bee·leer mee·yeem*
May I have…?	**…alabilir miyim?** *…ah·lah·bee·leer mee·yeem*
a kilo/half-kilo of…	**…dan *bir*/yarım kilo** *…dahn beer/yah·rihm kee·loh*
a liter/half-liter of…	**…dan *bir*/yarım litre** *…dahn beer/yah·rihm lee·treh*
a piece of…	**…bir parça** *…beer pahr·chah*
a slice of…	**…bir dilim** *…beer dee·leem*

In Turkey, there are a number of large supermarket and discount chains to shop in. They feature both local products as well as imported food. **Bakkal** (local grocery stores) can be found on just about every city block and offer enough to fill basic needs. There are also numerous specialty options: **çarşı** (small fruit and vegetable market), **balıkçı** (the fish store), and **kasap** (the butcher), in addition to the weekly **pazar** (neighborhood markets). In Istanbul be sure to visit the **Kapalı Çarşı** (covered bazaar) and the **Mısır Çarşısı** (spice bazaar).

YOU MAY HEAR...

Yardımcı olabilir miyim? _yahr·dihm·<u>jih</u>_ _oh·lah·bee·<u>leer</u> mee·yeem_ — Can I help you?

Ne istersiniz? _neh ees·<u>tehr</u>·see·neez_ — What would you like?

Başka bir şey? _bahsh·<u>kah</u> beer shay_ — Anything else?

...lira. _..._<u>lee</u>·rah_ — That's...lira.

More/Less.	**Daha fazla/az.** _dah·<u>hah</u> fahz·<u>lah</u>/<u>ahz</u>_	
How much?	**Ne kadar?** _<u>neh</u> kah·dahr_	
Where do I pay?	**Nereye ödeyeceğim?** _<u>neh</u>·reh·yeh ur·deh·yeh·<u>jeh</u>·yeem_	
May I have a bag?	**Bir çanta, alabilir miyim?** _beer chahn·<u>tah</u> ah·lah·bee·<u>leer</u> mee·yeem_	
I'm being helped.	**Yardım alıyorum.** _yahr·<u>dihm</u> ah·<u>lih</u>·yoh·room_	

For Conversion Tables, see page 181.

Measurements in Turkey are metric – and that applies to the weight of food too. If you tend to think in pounds and ounces, it's worth brushing up on what the metric equivalent is before you go shopping for fruit and veg in markets and supermarkets. Five hundred grams, or half a kilo, is a common quantity to order, and that converts to just over a pound (17.65 ounces, to be precise).

In the Kitchen

bottle opener	**şişe açacağı**	shee·_sheh_ ah·chah·jah·_ih_
bowls	**çanak**	chah·_nahk_
can opener	**konserve açacağı**	kon·sehr·_veh_ ah·chah·jah·_ih_
corkscrew	**şarap açacağı**	shah·_rahp_ ah·chah·jah·_ih_
cups	**fincan**	fihn·_jahn_
forks	**çatal**	chah·_tahl_
frying pan	**tava**	tah·_vah_
glasses	**bardak**	bahr·_dahk_
knives	**bıçak**	bih·_chahk_

measuring cup/spoon	**ölçü kabı/kaşığı** url·_chyu_ kah·_bih_/kah·shih·_ih_
napkin	**kağıt peçete** kah·_iht_ peh·_cheh_·teh
plates	**tabak** tah·_bakh_
pot	**çömlek** churm·_lehk_
saucepan	**tencere** tehn·_jeh_·reh
spatula	**spatula** spah·_too_·lah
spoons	**kaşık** kah·_shihk_

YOU MAY SEE…

SON KULLANMA TARİHİ…	expiration date…
KALORİ	calories
YAĞSIZ	fat free
BUZDOLABINDA SAKLAYINIZ	keep refrigerated
…UFAK BİR MİKTARINI İÇEREBİLİR	may contain small traces of…
EN GEÇ…TARİHİNE KADAR SATILABİLİR	may be sold until…
VEJETARYENLER İÇİN UYGUNDUR	suitable for vegetarians

Drinks

ESSENTIAL

May I see the wine list/drink menu, please?	**Şarap listesini/İçecek menüsünü görebilir miyim lütfen?** *shah·rahp lees·teh·see·nee/ ee·cheh·jehk meh·nyu·syu·nyu gur·reh·bee·leer mee·yeemlyut·fehn*
What do you recommend?	**Ne önerirsiniz?** *neh ur·neh·reer·see·neez*
I'd like a bottle/glass of red/white wine.	**Bir şişe/bardak kırmızı/beyaz şarap istiyorum.** *beer shee·sheh/bahr·dahk kihr·mih·zih/ beh·yahz shah·rahp ees·tee·yoh·room*
The house wine, please.	**Ev şarabı lütfen.** *ehv shah·rah·bih lyut·fehn*
Another bottle/glass, please.	**Bir şişe/bardak daha lütfen.** *beer shee·sheh/ bahr·dahk dah·hah lyut·fehn*
May I have a local beer?	**Yerel bir bira alabilir miyim?** *yeh·rehl beer bee·rah ah·lah·bee·leer mee·yeem*
Let me buy you a drink.	**Size bir içki ısmarlayayım.** *see·zeh beer eech·kee ihs·mahr·lah·yah·yihm*

Cheers!	**Şerefe!** sheh•reh•_feh_
A coffee/tea, please.	**Kahve/Çay lütfen.** kah•_hveh_/chie _lyut_•fehn
Black.	**Sütsüz.** syut•_syuz_
With milk.	**Sütlü.** syut•_lyu_
With sugar.	**Şekerli.** sheh•kehr•_lee_
With artificial sweetener.	**Yapay tatlandırıcılı.** yah•_pie_ taht•_lahn_•dih•rih•jih•lih
…please.	**…lütfen.** … _lyut_•fehn
Fruit juice	**Meyve suyu** may•_veh_ soo•yoo
Soda	**Soda** _soh_•dah
Sparkling/still wine	**Maden/Sade Su** mah•_dehn_/sah•_deh_ soo
Is the tap water safe to drink?	**Musluk suyu içilir mi?** moos•_look_ soo•_yoo_ ee•chee•_leer_ mee

Non-alcoholic Drinks

ayran ie•_rahn_	natural yogurt drink
kola _koh_•lah	soda
limonata lee•moh•_nah_•tah	lemonade

A number of non-alcoholic drinks are available in Turkey. Soft drinks and mineral water are easily found, though you may choose to enjoy a freshly-squeezed fruit juice, particularly in winter when citrus fruit is in season. And though Turkish coffee is internationally known, tea is more commonly drunk throughout the day. Black tea and herbal infusions are typical. Traditional drinks include **ayran** (yogurt drink), **boza** (fermented millet drink) and **sahlep** (wild orchid drink). **Ayran** is made by diluting yogurt and is often served with a pinch of salt added; it is a particularly refreshing drink in the summer. **Boza** and **sahlep** are only served in winter. **Boza** has a flavor similar to eggnog and **sahlep**, made from pulverized wild orchid roots, is sweet and is usually served with cinnamon sprinkled on top.

çay *chie*	tea
…kahve *…kah·hveh*	coffee…
kafeini alınmış *kah·feh·ee·nee ah·lihn·mihsh*	decaffeinated
sütlü *syut·lyu*	with milk
sütsüz *syut·syuz*	black
gazlı/gazsız maden suyu *gahz·lih/ gahz·sihz mah·dehn soo·yoo*	sparkling/still mineral water
salep *sah·lehp*	hot herbal drink
…suyu *…soo·yoo*	…juice
ananas *ah·nah·nahs*	pineapple
domates *doh·mah·tehs*	tomato
portakal *pohr·tah·kahl*	orange
süt *syut*	milk
sütlü meyve suyu *syut·lyu may·veh soo·yoo*	milk shake
şalgam suyu *shahl·gahm soo·yoo*	turnip juice

Aperitifs, Cocktails & Liqueurs

cin *jeen*	gin
erikli konyak *eh·reek·lee kohn·yahk*	plum brandy, slivovitz
kayısılı konyak *kah·yih·sih·lih kohn·yahk*	apricot brandy
konyak *kohn·yahk*	brandy
viski *vees·kee*	whisky
votka *voht·kah*	vodka

YOU MAY HEAR...

Size bir içki alabilir miyim? *see·zeh beer eech·kee ah·lah·bee·leer mee·yeem*	Can I get you a drink?
Sütlü/Şekerli? *syut·lyu/sheh·kehr·lee*	With milk/sugar?
Gazlı/Gazsız su? *gahz·lih/gahz·sihz soo*	Sparkling/Still water?

Beer

bira *bee·rah*	beer
fıçı *fih·chih*	draft [draught]
şişe *shee·sheh*	bottled

Foreign spirits are available in Turkey, but the national drink is
raki (aniseed liquor). Nearly 90-proof, it is usually drunk with a
bit of added water. Adding water turns it a milky-white, which has
earned the drink the nickname 'lion's milk.' Besides **raki**, Turkey also
produces very good brands of dry red and white wine and a few types of
beer, of which Efes is the most common.

Wine

beyaz şarap *beh·yahz shah·rahp*	white wine
kırmızı şarap *kihr·mih·zih shah·rahp*	red wine
köpüklü şarap *kur·pyuk·lyu shah·rahp*	sparkling wine
pembe şarap *pem·beh shah·rahp*	blush [rosé] wine
sek şarap *sehk shah·rahp*	dry wine
tatlı şarap *taht·lih shah·rahp*	sweet wine

A number of grape varieties are grown in Turkey and the country
has a long history of wine production. Each region specializes
in a few particular types of wine, depending on the grapes that are
grown there, so ask to try a local wine.

ahtapot *ah·tah·poht* — octopus

ahududu *ah·hoo·doo·doo* — raspberry

alabalık *ah·lah·bah·lihk* — trout

ananas *ah·nah·nahs* — pineapple

arnavut ciğeri *ahr·nah·voot jee·yeh·ree* — fried liver morsels

aşure *ah·shoo·reh* — sweet, cold soup made of mixed grains, beans and dried fruits

ayran *ie·rahn* — natural yogurt drink

ayva tatlısı *ie·vah taht·lih·sih* — baked quince slices in a syrup

az pişmiş *ahz peesh·meesh* — rare

baklava *bahk·lah·vah* — filo pastry filled with honey and pistachio nuts

bal *bahl* — honey

balık çorbası *bah·lihk chohr·bah·sih* — fish soup

beyaz peynir *beh·yahz pay·neer* — white cheese

beyaz şarap *beh·yahz shah·rahp* — white wine

bezelye *beh·zehl·yeh* — peas

biber *bee·behr* — pepper

bira *bee·rah* — beer

bonfile *bohn·fee·leh* — steak

boza *boh·zah* — a calorie-packed, sour-tasting drink made from fermented millet

böbrek *bur·brehk* — kidney

börek *bur·rehk* — hot filo pastries

but *boot* — leg

but eti *boot eh·tee* — rump

ciğer *jee·ehr* — liver

cin *jeen*	gin
çay *chie*	tea
Çerkez tavuğu *chehr·kehz tah·voo·oo*	Circassian chicken: boiled chicken with rice and nut sauce
Çınarcık usulü balık *chih·nahr·jihk oo·soo·lyu bah·lihk*	fried swordfish, sea bass and shrimp, served with mushrooms

There are several different denominations of eating and drinking establishments in Turkey. **Restoran** (restaurant) used to be a term reserved only for the finest establishments, but now many different types of places use the name. **Lokanta** (family-run restaurants) are more economical and unpretentious. The food in **lokanta** is generally prepared in advance rather than to order and is often served cafeteria-style. **Meyhane** (taverns) are generally smoke-filled, noisy taverns that serve wine, **raki** (aniseed liquor) and **meze** (appetizers), while **birahane** (beer hall) are typical beer halls. **Kebapci** (kebab joint), **dönerci** (doner joint) and **pideci** (a place specializing in **pide**, Turkish-style pizza) are the Turkish equivalents of fast-food places.

Keep in mind that not all restaurants will present you with a menu upon sitting down, but may instead offer you something seasonal or the specialty of the house or may just begin bringing **meze** (appetizers). In many establishments a tray is brought and you can select what you would like. Know that you are not obligated to accept every plate the waiter brings. Though many people choose to make an entire meal out of **meze** (appetizers), if you'd like to try some of the delicious main dish options, don't forget to save some room! Remember that fish is also sold by weight, so feel free to request that the waiter weigh it beforehand.

çırpma *chihrp·mah* — scrambled

çiğ köfte *chee kurf·teh* — raw meatballs made from ground meat and cracked wheat

çilek *chee·lehk* — strawberry

dana *dah·nah* — veal

dana pirzolası *dah·nah peer·zoh·lah·sih* — T-bone steak

deniz tarağı *deh·neez tah·rah·ih* — clams

dere otu *deh·reh oh·too* — dill

dolma *dohl·mah* — stuffed grape leaves

domates *doh·mah·tehs* — tomato

domuz *doh·mooz* — pork

ekmek *ehk·mehk* — bread

elma *ehl·mah* — apple

erik *eh·reek* — plum

erikli konyak *eh·reek·lee kohn·yahk* — plum brandy, slivovitz

et suyuna çorba *eht soo·yoo·nah chohr·bah* — consommé

ev şarabı *ehv shah·rah·bih* — house wine

fıçı *fih·chih* — draft [draught]

fileto *fee·leh·toh* — fillet

gazlı *gahz·lih* — sparkling water

gazlı maden suyu	*gahz·lih mah·dehn soo·yoo*	sparkling mineral water
gazsız	*gahz·sihz*	still water
gazsız maden suyu	*gahz·sihz mah·dehn soo·yoo*	still mineral water
greyfurt	*gray·foort*	grapefruit
havuç	*hah·vooch*	carrot
hıyar	*hih·yahr*	cucumber
hindi	*heen·dee*	turkey
ıstakoz	*ihs·tah·kohz*	lobster
içecek menüsünü	*ee·cheh·jehk meh·nyu·syu*	drink menu
içki	*eech·kee*	drink
imam bayıldı	*ee·mahm bah·yihl·dih*	eggplant [aubergine] stuffed with tomatoes and cooked in olive oil
istiridye	*ees·tee·reed·yeh*	oysters
iyi pişmiş	*ee·yee peesh·meesh*	well-done
jambon	*jahm·bohn*	ham
kabak	*kah·bahk*	zucchini [courgette]
kabak musakkası	*kah·bahk moo·sahk·kah·sih*	sautéed and fried eggplant [aubergine], green peppers, tomatoes, onions, zucchini [courgette] and ground meat

kabak tatlısı *kah·bahk taht·lih·sih*	baked pumpkin in a syrup
kadayıf *kah·dah·yihf*	shredded wheat dessert, similar to baklava
kafeini alınmış *kah·feh·ee·nee ah·lihn·mihsh*	decaffeinated
kahve *kah·hveh*	coffee
kalamar *kah·lah·mahr*	squid
karanfil *kah·rahn·feel*	cloves
karides *kah·ree·dehs*	shrimp [prawn]
karpuz *kahr·pooz*	watermelon
kaşar *kah·shahr*	hard cheese
katı *kah·tih*	boiled
kavun *kah·voon*	melon
kayısılı konyak *kah·yih·sih·lih kohn·yahk*	apricot brandy
kazandibi *kah·zahn·dee·bee*	oven-browned milk pudding
kekik *keh·keek*	thyme
kemikli et *keh·meek·lee eht*	cutlet
kereviz *keh·reh·veez*	celery
kılıç şiş *kih·lihch sheesh*	swordfish kebab grilled with bay leaves, tomatoes and green peppers
kırmızı biber *kih·mih·zih bee·behr*	chili
kırmızı şarap *kihr·mih·zih shah·rahp*	red wine
kızarmış ekmek *kih·zahr·mihsh ehk·mehk*	roasted bread
kimyon *keem·yohn*	cumin
kiraz *kee·rahz*	cherry
kişniş *keesh·neesh*	cilantro
kola *koh·lah*	soda
konyak *kohn·yahk*	brandy (cognac)
köpüklü şarap *kyu·pyuk·lyu shah·rahp*	sparkling wine
köpüksüz şarap *kyu·pyuk·syuz shah·rahp*	still wine
kremalı çorba *kreh·mah·lih chohr·bah*	cream soup

kuzu *koo-zoo* — lamb

kuzu dolması *koo-zoo dohl-mah-sih* — lamb stuffed with savory rice, liver and pistachios

kuzu güveç *koo-zoo gyu-vehch* — lamb stew with onions, garlic, potatoes, tomatoes and herbs

küçük yuvarlak ekmek *kyu-chyuk yoo-vahr-lahk ehk-mehk* — bread rolls

lahana *lah-hah-nah* — cabbage

leblebi *lehb-leh-bee* — roasted chick peas

limonata *lee-moh-nah-tah* — lemonade

lokum *loh-koom* — Turkish delight

lüfer *lyu-fehr* — bluefish

mantar *mahn-tahr* — mushroom

marmelat *mahr-meh-laht* — marmalade

marul *mah-rool* — lettuce

maydanoz *mie-dah-nohz* — parsley

meyve suyu *may-veh soo-yoo* — fruit juice

meze *meh-zeh* — appetizers

midye *meed-yeh* — mussels

morina balığı *moh-ree-nah bah-lih-ih* — cod

muhallebi *moo-hahl-leh-bee* — milk pudding

muz *mooz* — banana

nane *nah-neh* — mint

nar *nahr* — pomegranate

orta ateşte *ohr-tah ah-tehsh-teh* — medium

otlu peynir *oht-loo pay-neer* — herb cheese

ördek *ur-rdehk* — duck

patates *pah-tah-tehs* — potato

patates çorbası *pah-tah-tehs chohr-bah-sih* — potato soup

patlıcan *paht-lih-jahn* — eggplant [aubergine]

patlıcan salatası	*path·lih·jahn sah·lah·tah·sih*	eggplant [aubergine] salad
pembe şarap	*pem·beh shah·rahp*	blush [rosé] wine
pilaki	*pee·lah·kee*	beans in olive oil
pirinç	*pee·reench*	rice
pirzola	*peer·zoh·lah*	chops
pisi balığı	*pee·see bah·lih·ih*	plaice
portakal	*pohr·tah·kahl*	orange
portakal suyu	*pohr·tah·kahl soo·yoo*	orange juice
rakı	*rah·kih*	spirit made from distilled grapes and aniseed, similar to French pastis or Lebanese arak
reçel	*reh·chehl*	jam
ringa balığı	*reen·gah bah·lih·ih*	herring [whitebait]
safran	*sahf·rahn*	saffron
sahanda	*sah·hahn·dah*	fried
salep	*sah·lehp*	hot herbal drink
sarı şalgam	*sah·rih shahl·gahm*	rutabaga [swede]
sarmısak	*sahr·mih·sahk*	garlic
sebze çorbası	*sehb·zeh chohr·bah·sih*	vegetable soup
sek şarap	*sehk shah·rahp*	dry

sığır eti *sih•ihr eh•tee*	beef
sığır filetosu *sih•ihr fee•leh•toh•soo*	sirloin
soda *soh•dah*	soda
soğan *soh•ahn*	onion
soğan çorbası *soh•ahn chohr•bah•sih*	onion soup
sosis *soh•sees*	sausage
sülün *syu•lyun*	pheasant
süt *syut*	milk
sütlaç *syut•lahch*	rice pudding
sütlü *syut•lyu*	with milk
sütlü meyve suyu *syut•lyu may•veh soo•yoo*	milk shake
sütsüz *syut•syuz*	black
şalgam *shahl•gahm*	turnip
şalgam suyu *shahl•gahm soo•yoo*	turnip juice
şarap listesini *shah•rahp lees•teh•see*	wine list
şeftali *shehf•tah•lee*	peach
şeker *sheh•kehr*	sugar
şekerli *sheh•kehr•lee*	with sugar
şıra *shih•rah*	freshly pressed grape juice
şiş köfte *sheesh kurf•teh*	ground lamb croquettes on a skewer, grilled over charcoal

şişe *shee-<u>sheh</u>*	bottle
tarama *tah-rah-<u>mah</u>*	taramasalata, fish roe pâté
tatlı şarap *taht-<u>lih</u> shah-<u>rahp</u>*	sweet
tavşan *tahv-<u>shahn</u>*	rabbit
tavuk *tah-<u>vook</u>*	chicken
tavuk çorbası *tah-<u>vook</u> chohr-bah-sih*	chicken soup
tavuk göğsü *tah-<u>vook</u> gur-hsyu*	milk pudding with thin filaments of chicken breast
taze fasulye *tah-<u>zeh</u> fah-<u>sool</u>-yeh*	green beans
taze soğan *tah-<u>zeh</u> soh-<u>ahn</u>*	shallot [spring onion]
tereyağı *teh-<u>reh</u>-yah-ih*	butter
ton balığı *tohn bah-lih-ih*	tuna
tulum peyniri *too-<u>loom</u> pay-nee-<u>ree</u>*	goat cheese
türlü *tyur-<u>lyu</u>*	cooked mixed vegetables and beans, served hot
uskumru pilakisi *oos-<u>koom</u>-roo pee-lah-kee-see*	mackerel fried in olive oil, with potatoes, celery, carrots and garlic
üzüm *yu-<u>zyum</u>*	grapes
viski *vees-<u>kee</u>*	whisky
votka *voht-<u>kah</u>*	vodka
yapay tatlandırıcı *yah-<u>pie</u> taht-<u>lahn</u>-dih-rih-jih*	artificial sweetener
yoğurtlu kebab *yoh-oort-<u>loo</u> keh-<u>bahb</u>*	kebab on toasted bread with pureed tomatoes and seasoned yogurt
yumurta *yoo-<u>moor</u>-tah*	egg

People

ESSENTIAL

Hello.	**Merhaba.** _mehr_·hah·bah
Hi!	**Selam!** seh·_lahm_
How are you?	**Nasılsınız?** _nah_·sihl·sih·nihz
Fine, thanks.	**İyiyim, teşekkürler.** ee·_yee_·yeem teh·shehk·kyur·_lehr_
Excuse me!	**Afedersiniz!** _ahf_·eh·dehr·see·neez
Do you speak English?	**İngilizce biliyor musunuz?** een·gee·_leez_·jeh bee·_lee_·yohr moo·soo·nooz
What's your name?	**İsminiz nedir?** ees·mee·_neez_ neh·deer
My name is…	**İsmim…** ees·_meem_…
Pleased to meet you.	**Tanıştığımıza memnun oldum.** tah·nihsh·tih·ih·mih·_zah_ mehm·_noon_ ohl·doom
Where are you from?	**Nerelisiniz?** _neh_·reh·lee·see·neez
I'm from the U.S./U.K.	**Amerikadanım/Birleşik Krallıktanım.** ah·meh·_ree_·kah·dah·nihm/beer·leh·_sheek_ krahl·lihk·_tah_·nihm
What do you do?	**Ne iş yapıyorsunuz?** _neh_ eesh yah·_pih_·yohr·soo·nooz
I work for…	**…için çalışıyorum.** …ee·_cheen_ chah·lih·_shih_·yoh·room
I'm a student.	**öğrenciyim.** ur·rehn·_jee_·eem
I'm retired.	**Emekliyim.** eh·mehk·_lee_·yeem
Do you like…?	**…sever misiniz?** …seh·_vehr_ mee·see·neez
Goodbye. (said by departing persons)	**Hoşçakalın.** hosh·_chah_ kah·lihn

Goodbye. (said by second person staying behind) | **Güle güle.** *gyu·leh gyu·leh*

See you later. | **Tekrar görüşmek üzere.** *tehk·rahr gur·ryush·mehk yu·zeh·reh*

When formally addressing someone, it is polite to use the person's first name followed by either **Hanım** (polite address for women) or **Bey** (polite address for men). So Ali and his wife Binnur would be addressed as Ali Bey and Binnur Hanım, respectively. **Bay** (polite address for male foreigners) and **Bayan** (polite address for female foreigners) are also used, particularly for non-Muslims. In business settings, **Sayin** (polite address for men and women in a business setting) is commonly used followed by the last name. For example, Ali Kandemir would be addressed as Sayin Kandemir.

Language Difficulties

Do you speak English? | **İngilizce biliyor musunuz?** *een·gee·leez·jeh bee·lee·yohr moo·soo·nooz*

Does anyone here speak English? | **Burada İngilizce konuşan biri var mı?** *boo·rah·dah een·gee·leez·jeh koh·noo·shahn bee·ree vahr mih*

I don't speak Turkish. | **Türkçe bilmiyorum.** *tyurk·cheh beel·mee·yoh·room*

Can you speak more slowly? | **Daha yavaş konuşur musunuz lütfen?** *dah·hah yah·vahsh koh·noo·shoor moo·soo·nooz lyut·fehn*

Can you repeat that? | **Tekrar eder misiniz lütfen?** *tekh·rahr eh·dehr mee·see·neez lyut·fehn*

Excuse me?	**Efendim?** *eh·fehn·deem*	
What was that?	**O neydi?** *oh nay·dee*	
Write it down, please.	**Lütfen yazar mısınız.** *lyut·fehn yah·zahr mih·sih·nihz*	
Can you translate this for me?	**Bunu benim için tercüme eder misiniz?** *boo·noo beh·neem ee·cheen tehr·jyu·meh eh·dehr mee·see·neez*	
What does this/that mean?	**Bu/O ne demek?** *boo/oh neh deh·mehk*	
I understand.	**Anladım.** *ahn·lah·dihm*	
I don't understand.	**Anlamadım.** *ahn·lah·mah·dihm*	
Do you understand?	**Anladınız mı?** *anh·lah·dih·nihz mih*	

YOU MAY HEAR…

Sadece çok az İngilizce konuşuyorum. *sah·deh·jeh chohk ahz een·geh·leez·jeh koh·noo·shoo·yoh·room*	I only speak a little English.
İngilizce konuşmuyorum. *een·gee·leez·jeh koh·noosh·moo·yoh·room*	I don't speak English.

Making Friends

Hello.	**Merhaba.** _mehr·hah·bah_
Hi!	**Selam!** _seh·lahm_
Good morning.	**Günaydın.** _gyu·nie·dihn_
Good afternoon.	**İyi günler.** _ee·yee gyun·lehr_
Good evening.	**İyi akşamlar.** _ee·yee ahk·shahm·lahr_
My name is…	**İsmim…** _ees·meem_…
What's your name?	**İsminiz nedir?** _ees·mee·neez neh·deer_
I'd like to introduce you to…	**Sizi…ile tanıştırmak istiyorum.** _see·zee…ee·leh tah·nihsh·tihr·mahk ees·tee·yoh·room_
Nice to meet you.	**Tanıştığımıza memnun oldum.** _tah·nihsh·tih·ih·mih·zah mehm·noon ohl·doom_
How are you?	**Nasılsınız?** _nah·sihl·sih·nihz_
Fine, thanks.	**İyiyim, teşekkürler.** _ee·yee·yeem teh·shehk·kyur·lehr_
And you?	**Siz?** _seez_

> Turkish has both a formal 'you', **siz**, and an informal 'you', **sen**. The formal 'you' is used when speaking with strangers and out of respect, for example, when talking with someone older than you. The informal 'you' can be used with people you know or people younger than you. Though older people maintain this distinction, many young people start using the informal 'you' right away.

Travel Talk

I'm here…	**…amacıyla buradayım.** …_ah·mah·jihy·lah boo·rah·dah·yihm_
on business	**İş** _eesh_
on vacation	**Tatil** _tah·teel_

studying	**Okumak**	*oh·koo·mahk*
I'm staying for…	**…için kalıyorum.**	*…ee·cheen kah·lih·yoh·room*
I've been here…	**…burdayım.**	*…boor·dah·yihm*
a day	**Bir gündür**	*beer gyun·dyur*
a week	**Bir haftadır**	*beer hahf·tah·dihr*
a month	**Bir aydır**	*beer ie·dihr*
Where are you from?	**Nerelisiniz?**	*neh·reh·lee·see·neez*
I'm from…	**…denim.**	*…deh·neem*

Personal

Who are you with?	**Kiminlesiniz?**	*kee·meen·leh·see·neez*
I'm on my own.	**Tek başımayım.**	*tehk bah·shih·mah·yihm*
I'm with…	**…ile birlikteyim.**	*…ee·leh beer·leek·teh·yeem*
my husband/wife	**Kocam/Karım**	*koh·jahm/kah·rihm*
my boyfriend/	**Erkek/Kız arkadaşım**	
girlfriend		*ehr·kehk/kihz ahr·kah·dah·shihm*
a friend	**Bir arkadaş**	*beer ahr·kah·dahsh*
a colleague	**Bir meslektaş**	*beer mehs·lehk·tahsh*
When's your birthday?	**Doğum gününüz ne zaman?**	*doh·oom gyu·nyu·nyuz neh zah·mahn*
How old are you?	**Kaç yaşındasınız?**	*kahch yah·shihn·dah·sih·nihz*

I'm…	**…yaşındayım.** …yah·shihn·_dah_·yihm
Are you married?	**Evli misiniz?** ehv·_lee_ mee·see·neez
I'm single.	**Bekârım.** beh·_kah_·rihm
I'm married.	**Evliyim.** ehv·_lee_·yeem
I'm divorced.	**Boşanmışım.** boh·shan·_nih_·shihm
I'm separated.	**Ayrıyım.** ie·_rih_·yihm
I'm in a relationship.	**Beraberliğim var.** beh·rah·behr·lee·_eem_ vahr
I'm widowed.	**Dulum.** _doo_·loom
Do you have children/ grandchildren?	**Çocuğunuz/Torununuz var mı?** choh·joo·oo·_nooz_/ toh·roo·noo·_nooz_ vahr mih

For Numbers, see page 176.

Work & School

What do you do?	**Ne iş yapıyorsunuz?** _neh_ eesh yah·_pih_·yohr·soo·nooz
What are you studying?	**Ne okuyorsunuz?** _neh_ oh·_koo_·yohr·soo·nooz
I'm studying…	**…okuyorum.** …oh·_koo_·yoh·room
I work full/part time.	**Tam/Yarım zamanlı çalışıyorum.** tahm/yah·_rihm_ zah·mahn·lih chah·lih·shih·yoh·room
I'm between jobs.	**İşten yeni ayrıldım.** eesh·_tehn_ yeh·_nee_ ie·rihl·_deem_
I work at home.	**Evde çalışıyorum.** ehv·_deh_ chah·lih·_shih_·yoh·room

Who do you work for?	**Kimin için çalışıyorsunuz?** *kee·<u>meen</u> ee·cheen chah·lih·<u>shih</u>·yohr·soo·nooz*
I work for…	**…için çalışıyorum.** …*ee·<u>cheen</u> chah·lih·<u>shih</u>·yoh·room*
Here's my business card.	**Buyrun, kartvizitim.** *<u>booy</u>·roon <u>cahrt</u>·vee·zee·<u>teem</u>*

For Business Travel, see page 147.

Weather

What is the weather forecast for tomorrow?	**Yarın için hava tahmini nasıl?** *<u>yah</u>·rihn ee·cheen hah·<u>vah</u> tah·mee·<u>nee</u> nah·sihl*
What beautiful/terrible weather!	**Ne kadar güzel/kötü bir hava!** *neh kah·dahr gyu·<u>zehl</u>/kur·<u>tyu</u> beer hah·<u>vah</u>*
It's cool/warm.	**Serin/Ilık.** *seh·<u>reen</u>/ih·<u>lihk</u>*
It's rainy/sunny.	**Yağmurlu/Güneşli.** *yah·moor·<u>loo</u>/gyu·nehsh·<u>lee</u>*
It's snowy/icy.	**Karlı/Buzlu.** *kahr·<u>lih</u>/booz·<u>loo</u>*
Do I need a jacket/ an umbrella?	**Monta/Şemsiyeye ihtiyacım var mı?** *mohn·<u>tah</u>/ shehm·see·yeh·<u>yeh</u> eeh·tee·yah·<u>jihm</u> vahr mih*

For Temperature, see page 182.

ESSENTIAL

Would you like to go out for a drink/meal?	**Dışarı çıkıp birşeyler içmek/yemek ister misiniz?** *dih·shah·rih chih·kihp beer shay·lehr eech·mehk/yeh·mehk ees·tehr mee·see·neez*
What are your plans for tonight/tomorrow?	**Bu gece/yarın için planınız ne?** *boo geh·jeh/ yah·rinn ee·cheen plah·nih·nihz neh*
Can I have your number?	**Telefon numaranızı öğrenebilir miyim?** *teh·leh·fohn noo·mah·rah·nih·zih ur·reh·neh·bee·leer mee·yeem*
Can I join you?	**Size katılabilir miyim?** *see·zeh kah·tih·lah·bee·leer mee·yeem*
Let me buy you a drink.	**Size bir içki ısmarlayayım.** *see·zeh beer eech·kee ihs·mahr·lah·yah·yihm*
I like you.	**Sizden hoşlanıyorum.** *seez·dehn hohsh·lah·nih·yoh·room*
I love you.	**Sizi seviyorum.** *see·zee seh·vee·yoh·room*

The Dating Game

Would you like to...?	**...ister misiniz?** *...ees·tehr mee·see·neez*
go out for coffee	**Kahve içmeye gitmek** *kah·veh eech·meh·yeh geet·mehk*
go for a drink	**İçki içmeye gitmek** *eech·kee eech·meh·yeh geet·mehk*
go for a meal	**Yemeğe çıkmak** *yeh·meh·yeh chihk·mahk*
You're very attractive!	**Çok iyi görünüyorsunuz!** *chohk ee·yee gur·ryu·nyu·yohr·soo·nooz*

What are your plans for…?	**…için planınız ne?** … _ee•cheen plah•nih•nihz neh_
tonight	**Bu gece** _boo geh•jeh_
tomorrow	**Yarın** _yah•rihn_
this weekend	**Bu haftasonu** _boo hahf•tah•soh•noo_
Where would you like to go?	**Nereye gitmek istersiniz?** _neh•reh•yeh geet•mehk ees•tehr•see•neez_
I'd like to go to…	**…gitmek isterim.** … _geet•mehk ees•teh•reem_
Do you like…?	**…ister misiniz?** … _ees•tehr mee•see•neez_
Can I have your number/e-mail?	**Numaranızı/Posta adresinizi alabilir miyim?** _noo•mah•rah•nih•zih/pohs•tah ahd•reh•see•nee•zee ah•lah•bee•leer mee•yeem_
Are you on Facebook/Twitter?	**Facebook/Twitter'da mısın?** _Facebook/Twitter'dah mih•sihn_
Can I join you?	**Size katılabilir miyim?** _see•zeh kah•tih•lah•bee•leer mee•yeem_
Shall we go somewhere quieter?	**Daha sakin bir yere gidelim mi?** _dah•hah sah•keen beer yeh•reh gee•deh•leem mee_

For Communications, see page 53.

Accepting & Rejecting

Thank you. I'd love to.	**Teşekkür ederim. Sevinirim.** *teh·shehk·kyur eh·deh·reem seh·vee·nee·reem*
Where shall we meet?	**Nerede buluşalım?** *neh·reh·deh boo·loo·shah·lihm*
I'll meet you at the bar/ your hotel.	**Sizi barda/otelinizde bulurum.** *see·zee bahr·dah/ oh·teh·lee·neez·deh boo·loo·room*
I'll come by at…	**…uğrarım.** *…oo·rah·rihm*
What's your address?	**Adresin nedir?** *ahd·reh·seen neh·deer*
Thank you, but I'm busy.	**Teşekkür ederim ama meşgulüm.** *teh·shehk·kyur eh·deh·reem ah·mah mehsh·goo·lyum*
I'm not interested.	**İlgilenmiyorum.** *eel·gee·lehn·mee·yoh·room*
Leave me alone!	**Beni yalnız bırakın lütfen!** *beh·nee yahl·nihz bih·rah·kihn lyut·fehn*
Stop bothering me!	**Canımı sıkmayı kesin!** *jah·nih·mih sihk·mah·yih keh·seen*

For Time, see page 177.

Getting Intimate

Can I hug/kiss you?	**Sizi kucaklayabilir/öpebilir miyim?** *see-zee koo-jahk-lah-yah-bee-leer/ur-peh-bee-leer mee-yeem*
Yes.	**Evet.** *eh-veht*
No.	**Hayır.** *hah-yihr*
Stop!	**Dur!** *door*

Sexual Preferences

Are you gay?	**Gey misiniz?** *gay mee-see-neez*
I'm heterosexual.	**Ben karşı cinse ilgi duyarım.** *behn kahr-shih jeen-seh eel-gee doo-yah-rihm*
I'm homosexual.	**Eşcinselim.** *ehsh-jeen-seh-leem*
I'm bisexual.	**Biseksüelim.** *beeh-sehk-syu-eh-leem*
Do you like men/ women?	**Erkeklerden/Kadınlardan hoşlanır mısınız?** *ehr-kehk-lehr-dehn/kah-dihn-lahr-dahn hosh-lah-nihr mih-sih-nihz*

Leisure Time

ESSENTIAL

Where's the tourist office?	**Turist danışma bürosu nerede?** *too•reest dah•nihsh•mah byu•roh•soo neh•reh•deh*
What are the main points of interest?	**Başlıca ilginç yerler nelerdir?** *bahsh•lih•jah eel•geench yehr•lehr neh•lehr•deer*
Do you have tours in English?	**İngilizce turlarınız var mı?** *een•geh•leez•jeh toor•lah•rih•nihz vahr mih*
Can I have a map/ guide?	**Harita/Rehber alabilir miyim?** *hah•ree•tah/ reh•ber ah•lah•bee•leer mee•yeem*

Tourist Information

Do you have any information on...?	**...hakkında bir bilginiz var mı?** *...hahk•kihn•dah beer beel•gee•neez vahr mih*
Can you recommend...?	**...önerebilir misiniz?** *...ur•neh•reh•bee•leer mee•see•neez*
a boat trip	**Bir gemi gezisi** *beer geh•mee geh•zee•see*
an excursion	**Bir gezinti** *beer geh•zeen•tee*
a sightseeing tour	**Bir tur** *beer toor*

Turizm Danışma Bürosu (tourist information offices) are located in cities throughout Turkey. In smaller cities, the office is often located in or near the main square. Big cities usually have several offices. The tourist office can provide maps and information about the area and help in making reservations. Travel agents are also helpful in assisting with information and can often offer good rates on hotel reservations.

On Tour

I'd like to go on the tour to…	**…turla gitmek istiyorum.** … _toor_·lah geet·_mehk_ ees·_tee_·yoh·room
When's the next tour?	**Bir sonraki tur ne zaman?** beer _sohn_·rah·kee toor _neh_ zah·mahn
Are there tours in English?	**İngilizce turlar var mı?** een·gee·_leez_·jeh toor·_lahr_ _vahr_ mih
Is there an English-speaking guide?	**İngilizce konuşan bir rehber var mı?** een·gee·_leez_·jeh koh·noo·_shahn_ beer reh·_behr_ _vahr_ mih
What time do we leave/return?	**Saat kaçta ayrılacağız/döneceğiz?** sah·_aht_ kahch·_tah_ ie·rih·lah·_jah_·ihz/dur·neh·_jeh_·eez
We'd like to have a look at the…	**…bakmak istiyoruz.** … bahk·_mahk_ ees·_tee_·yoh·rooz
Can we stop here…?	**Burada…durabilir miyiz?** _boo_·rah·dah… doo·rah·bee·_leer_ mee·yeez
to take photographs	**fotoğraf çekmek için** foh·toh·_rahf_ chehk·_mehk_ ee·cheen
for souvenirs	**hediyelik eşya satın almak için** heh·dee·yeh·_leek_ ehsh·_yah_ sah·_tihn_ ahl·_mahk_ ee·cheen
to use the restroom [toilet]	**tuvalete gitmek için** too·vah·leh·_teh_ geet·_mehk_ ee·_cheen_
Is there access for the disabled?	**Özürlüler girebilir mi?** ur·zyur·lyu·_lehr_ gee·reh·bee·_leer_ mee

For Tickets, see page 19.

Seeing the Sights

Where is…?	**…nerede?** … _neh_·reh·deh
the battleground	**Muharebe meydanı** moo·hah·reh·_beh_ may·dah·nih
the botanical garden	**Botanik bahçesi** boh·tah·_neek_ bah·cheh·_see_
the castle	**Kale** kah·_leh_

the downtown area	**Kent merkezi** kehnt mehr·keh·<u>zee</u>
the fountain	**Çeşme** chehsh·<u>meh</u>
the library	**Kütüphane** kyu·tyup·hah·<u>neh</u>
the market	**Pazar** pah·<u>zahr</u>
the museum	**Müze** myu·<u>zeh</u>
the old town	**Eski kent** ehs·<u>kee</u> kehnt
the palace	**Saray** sah·<u>rie</u>
the park	**Park** pahrk
the shopping area	**Alış veriş merkezi** ah·<u>lihsh</u> veh·<u>reesh</u> mehr·keh·<u>zee</u>
the town square	**Kasaba meydanı** kah·sah·<u>bah</u> may·dah·<u>nih</u>
Can you show me on the map?	**Bana haritada gösterebilir misiniz?** bah·<u>nah</u> hah·<u>ree</u>·tah·dah gurs·teh·reh·bee·<u>leer</u> mee·see·neez
It's...	**...-dir.** ...deer
amazing	**Hayret verici** hie·<u>reht</u> veh·ree·<u>jee</u>
beautiful	**Güzel** gyu·<u>zehl</u>
boring	**Sıkıcı** sih·kih·<u>jih</u>
interesting	**İlginç** eel·<u>ginch</u>
magnificent	**Muhteşem** mooh·teh·<u>shehm</u>
romantic	**Romantik** roh·mahn·<u>teek</u>
strange	**Şaşırtıcı** shah·shihr·tih·<u>jih</u>
stunning	**Çarpıcı** chahr·pih·<u>jih</u>

terrible	**Berbat** behr·_baht_
ugly	**Çirkin** cheer·_keen_
I like it.	**Beğendim.** beh·yehn·_deem_
I don't like it.	**Beğenmedim.** beh·_yehn_·meh·deem

For Asking Directions, see page 36.

Religious Sites

Where's…?	**…nerede?** … _neh_·reh·deh
the cathedral	**Katedral** kah·tehd·_rahl_
the Catholic/	**Katolik/Protestan kilisesi** kah·toh·_leek_/
Protestant church	proh·tehs·_tahn_ kee·lee·seh·_see_
the mosque	**Cami** jah·_mee_
the shrine	**Mabet** mah·_baht_
the synagogue	**Havra** _hahv_·rah
the temple	**Tapınak** tah·pih·_nahk_
What time is mass/	**Ayin/İbadet saat kaçta?** ah·_yihn_/ee·bah·_deht_
the service?	sah·_aht_ kahch·tah

Turkey is a Muslim country and the majority of the population belongs to the Sunni branch of Islam. It is, however, a secular state. Individuals are guaranteed freedom of religion by the constitution, which at the same time protects religious groups. The constitution also specifies that the political system must be explicitly religion-free. That means religious groups may not form political parties or establish schools based on a particular faith. Turkey also prohibits wearing religious garments, such as head covers, in all government buildings as well as schools and universities.

Shopping

ESSENTIAL

Where is the market/ mall [shopping centre]?	**Market/Alış veriş merkezi nerede?**	*mahr·keht/ah·lihsh veh·reesh mehr·keh·zee neh·reh·deh*
I'm just looking.	**Sadece bakıyorum.**	*sah·deh·jeh bah·kih·yoh·room*
Can you help me?	**Bana yardım edebilir misiniz?**	*bah·nah yahr·dihm eh·deh·bee·leer mee·see·neez*
I'm being helped.	**Yardım alıyorum.**	*yahr·dihm ah·lih·yoh·room*
How much?	**Ne kadar?**	*neh kah·dahr*
That one.	**Şunu.**	*shoo·noo*
That's all, thanks.	**Hepsi bu, teşekkürler.**	*hehp·see boo teh·shehk·kyur·lehr*
Where do I pay?	**Nereye ödeyeceğim?**	*neh·reh·yeh ur·deh·yeh·jeh·yeem*

| I'll pay in cash/by credit card. | **Nakit/Kredi kartı ile ödeyeceğim.** *nah-keet/ kreh-dee kahr-tih ee-leh ur-deh-yeh-jeh-yeem* |
| A receipt, please. | **Fatura lütfen.** *fah-too-rah lyut-fehn* |

One thing not to miss while in Turkey is the weekly **pazar** (neighborhood market), found outside in almost every town throughout the country. In Istanbul, be sure to visit the **Kapali Çarşı** (Covered market or Grand Bazaar), the **Mısır Çarşısı** (Spice Market) and the **Balık Pazarı** (Fish Bazaar). Beware of pickpockets though. They are prevalent in these places, so tourists should pay attention their valuables.

At the Shops

Where is...?	**...nerede?** *...neh-reh-deh*
the antique store	**Antikacı** *ahn-tee-kah-jih*
the bakery	**Fırın** *fih-rihn*
the bank	**Banka** *bahn-kah*
the bookstore	**Kitapçı** *kee-tahp-chih*
the clothing store	**Elbise mağazası** *ehl-bee-seh mah-ah-zah-sih*
the delicatessen	**Şarküteri** *shahr-kyu-teh-ree*
the department store	**Mağaza** *mah-ah-zah*
the gift shop	**Hediyelik eşya dükkanı** *heh-dee-yeh-leek ehsh-yah dyuk-kah-nih*
the health food store	**Sağlıklı yiyecekler dükkanı** *sah-lihk-lih yee-yeh-jehk-lehr dyuk-kah-nih*

the jeweler	**Kuyumcu** *koo·yoom·joo*
the liquor store [off-licence]	**Tekel bayii** *teh·kehl bah·yee·ee*
the market	**Market** *mahr·keht*
the pastry shop	**Pastane** *pahs·tah·neh*
the pharmacy [chemist]	**Eczane** *ehj·zah·neh*
the produce [grocery] store	**Manav** *mah·nahv*
the shoe store	**Ayakkabıcı** *ah·yahk·kah·bih·jih*
the shopping mall [centre]	**Alış veriş merkezi** *ah·lihsh veh·reesh mehr·keh·zee*
the souvenir store	**Hediyelik eşya dükkanı** *heh·dee·yeh·leek ehsh·yah dyuk·kah·nih*
the supermarket	**Süpermarket** *syu·pehr·mahr·keht*
the tobacconist	**Tütüncü** *tyu·tyun·jyu*
the toy store	**Oyuncakçı** *oh·yoon·jahk·chih*

Ask an Assistant

When does the... open/close?	**...ne zaman açılıyor/kapanıyor?** ...*neh zah•mahn ah•chih•lih•yohr/kah•pah•nih•yohr*
Where is...?	**...nerede?** ...*neh•reh•deh*
the cashier [cash desk]	**Kasa** *kah•sah*
the escalator	**Yürüyen merdiven** *yyu•ryu•yehn mehr•dee•vehn*
the elevator [lift]	**Asansör** *ah•sahn•surr*
the fitting room	**Giyinme kabinleri** *gee•yeen•meh kah•been•leh•ree*
the store directory [guide]	**Mağaza rehberi** *mah•ah•zah rehh•beh•ree*
Can you help me?	**Bana yardım edebilir misiniz?** *bah•nah yahr•dihm eh•deh•bee•leer mee•see•neez*
I'm just looking.	**Sadece bakıyorum.** *sah•deh•jeh bah•kih•yoh•room*
I'm being helped.	**Yardım alıyorum.** *yahı•dihm ah•lih•yoh•room*
Do you have any...?	**...var mı?** ...*vahr mih*
Can you show me...?	**...gösterebilir misiniz?** ...*gurs•teh•reh•bee•leer mee•see•neez*
Can you ship/wrap it?	**Kargoyla yollayabilir/Paketleyebilir misiniz?** *kahr•gohy•lah yohl•lah•yah•bee•leer/ pah•keht•leh•yeh•bee•leer mee•see•neez*

YOU MAY HEAR...

Yardımcı olabilir miyim? *yahr•dihm•jih oh•lah•bee•leer mee•yeem*	Can I help you?
Bir dakika. *beer dah•kee•kah*	One moment.
Ne istersiniz? *neh ees•tehr•see•neez*	What would you like?
Başka bir şey? *bahsh•kah beer shay*	Anything else?

| How much? | **Ne kadar?** _neh_ kah•dahr |
| That's all, thanks. | **Hepsi bu, teşekkürler.** hehp•see _boo_ teh•shehk•_kyur_•lehr |

For Meals & Cooking, see page 73.

Personal Preferences

I'd like something…	**…bir şey istiyorum.** …beer _shay_ ees•_tee_•yoh•room
cheap/expensive	**Ucuz/Pahalı** oo•_jooz_/pah•_hah_•lih
larger/smaller	**Daha büyük/küçük** dah•_hah_ byu•yyuk/kyu•chyuk
from this region	**Bu çevreden** boo chehv•reh•_dehn_
Is it real?	**Hakiki mi?** hah•kee•_kee_ mee
Could you show me this/that?	**Bunu/Onu bana gösterebilir misiniz?** boo•_noo_/ oh•noo bah•nah gyus•teh•reh•bee•_leer_ mee•see•neez
That's not quite what I want.	**Bu tam istediğim gibi değil.** boo _tahm_ ees•teh•dee•_yeem_ gee•bee _deh_•yeel
I don't like it.	**Beğenmedim.** beh•_yehn_•meh•deem
That's too expensive.	**Çok pahalı.** chohk pah•_hah_•lih
I'd like to think about it.	**Biraz düşünmek istiyorum.** _bee_•rahz dyu•shyun•_mehk_ ees•_tee_•yoh•room
I'll take it.	**Alıyorum.** ah•_lih_•yoh•room

YOU MAY HEAR...

Nasıl ödeyeceksiniz? *nah·sihl ur·deh·yeh·jehk·see·neez*

How are you paying?

İşlem onaylanmadı/kabul edilmedi. *eesh·lehm oh·nie·lahn·mah·dih/kah·bool eh·deel·meh·dee*

This transaction has not been approved/accepted.

Başka bir kimlik kartınızı görebilir miyim? *bahsh·kah beer keem·leek kahr·tih·nih·zih gur·reh·bee·leer mee·yeem*

May I see another ID card?

Sadece nakit lütfen. *sah·deh·jeh nah·keet lyut·fehn*

Cash only, please.

Bozuğunuz yok mu? *boh·zoo·oo·nooz yohk moo*

Do you have any smaller change?

Major credit cards are commonly accepted, though not everywhere. It is a good idea to have some cash on hand, just in case. Note that some establishments also pass on the credit-processing costs, usually between 3-6%, as a surcharge.

Paying & Bargaining

How much?	**Ne kadar?** _neh_ kah·dahr
I'll pay by…	**…ile ödeyeceğim.** …ee·_leh_ ur·deh·yeh·_jeh_·yeem
in cash	**Nakit** nah·_keet_
by credit card	**Kredi kartı ile** kreh·_dee_ kahr·_tih_ ee·leh
by traveler's check [cheque]	**Seyahat çeki** seh·yah·_haht_ cheh·_kee_
A receipt, please.	**Fatura lütfen.** fah·_too_·rah _lyut_·fehn
That's too much.	**Çok pahalı.** _chohk_ pah·hah·_lih_
I'll give you…	**…veririm.** …veh·_ree_·reem
I only have…lira.	**Sadece…liram var.** _sah_·deh·jeh…lee·_rahm_ vahr
Is that your best price?	**En son fiyat bu mu?** ehn sohn fee·_yaht_ _boo_ moo
Give me a discount.	**Bana bir indirim yapın.** bah·_nah_ beer een·deer·_reem_ yah·pihn

For Numbers, see page 176.

Making a Complaint

I'd like…	**…istiyorum.** …ees·_tee_·yoh·room
to exchange this	**Bunu değiştirmek** boo·_noo_ deh·yeesh·teer·_mehk_
to return this	**Geri vermek** geh·_ree_ vehr·_mehk_
a refund	**Paramı geri** pah·rah·_mih_ geh·_ree_
to see the manager	**Müdürü görmek** myu·dyu·_ryu_ gurr·_mehk_

Services

Can you recommend…?	**…önerebilir misiniz?**	…ur·neh·reh·bee·<u>leer</u> mee·see·neez
a barber	**Berber** behr·behr	
a dry cleaner	**Kuru temizleyici** koo·<u>roo</u> teh·mceez·leh·yee·<u>jee</u>	
a hairdresser	**Kuaför** koo·ah·<u>furr</u>	
a laundromat [launderette]	**Çamaşırhane** chah·mah·shihr·hah·<u>neh</u>	
a nail salon	**Güzellik salonu** gyu·zehl·<u>leek</u> sah·loh·<u>noo</u>	
a spa	**Kaplıca** <u>kahp</u>·lih·jah	
a travel agency	**Seyahat acentası** seh·yah·<u>haht</u> ah·jehn·tah·<u>sih</u>	
Can you…this?	**Bunu…misiniz?** boo·<u>noo</u>…mee·see·neez	
alter	**değiştirebilir** deh·yeesh·tee·reh·bee·<u>leer</u>	
clean	**temizleyebilir** teh·meez·leh·yeh·bee·<u>leer</u>	
mend	**yamalayabilir** yah·mah·lah·yah·bee·<u>leer</u>	
press	**ütüleyebilir** yu·tyu·leh·yeh·bee·<u>leer</u>	
When will it be ready?	**Ne zaman hazır olacak?** neh zah·<u>mahn</u> hah·<u>zihr</u> oh·lah·<u>jahk</u>	

Hair & Beauty

I'd like…	…istiyorum. ….ees·<u>tee</u>·yoh·room
an appointment for today/tomorrow	**Bugün/Yarın için bir randevu** <u>boo</u>·gyun/<u>yah</u>·rihn ee·cheen beer rahn·deh·<u>voo</u>
some color	**Boyama** boh·yah·<u>mah</u>
some highlights	**Röfle** rurf·<u>leh</u>
my hair styled	**Saç şekillendirme** <u>sahch</u> sheh·keel·lehn·deer·<u>meh</u>
a haircut	**Kestirmek** kehs·teer·<u>mehk</u>
a trim	**Uçlarından aldırmak** ooch·lah·rihn·<u>dahn</u> ahl·dihr·<u>mahk</u>
Don't cut it too short.	**Çok kısa kesmeyin.** chohk kih·<u>sah</u> <u>kehs</u>·meh·yeen
Shorter here.	**Burayı kısaltın.** boo·rah·<u>yih</u> kih·<u>sahl</u>·tihn
an eyebrow/bikini wax	**Kaş aldırma/Ağda** <u>kahsh</u> ahl·dih·mah/<u>ah</u>·<u>dah</u>

Turkey is an excellent destination for visiting spas. There are many throughout the country and are recommended by the Turks as a means of natural therapy or a cure for certain ailments. There are many different treatments to enjoy: bathing in thermal springs, mud baths, wraps, massages and, the most famous of all, the Turkish bath. Turkish baths are a type of wet sauna or steam bath and have been known in Turkey for centuries. The concept was only exported to Europe around the mid-1800s.

If you are looking for a unique experience, consider visiting the hot springs in Kangal, located in the Sivas province, in Central Anatolia. In this thermal bath, mineral water flows in from five different springs and along with it so do innumerable small fish (small meaning about 1 to 5 inches long). Bathing with them is said to cure many skin illnesses.

125

a facial	**Yüz masajı** yyuz mah•sah•_jih_
a manicure/pedicure	**Manikür/Pedikür** mah•nee•_kyur_/peh•dee•_kyur_
a (sports) massage	**Bir (spor) masajı** beer (spohr) mah•sah•_jih_
Do you do…?	**…yapar mısınız?** …yah•_pahr_ mih•sih•nihz
acupuncture	**Akupunktur** ah•koo•poonk•_toor_
aromatherapy	**Aroma terapi** ah•_roh_•mah teh•rah•_pee_
oxygen treatment	**Oksijen tedavisi** ohk•see•_jehn_ teh•dah•vee•_see_
Is there a sauna?	**Sauna var mı?** sah•oo•_nah_ _vahr_ mih

Antiques

How old is this?	**Bu ne kadar eski?** boo _neh_ kah•dahr ehs•_kee_
Will I have problems with customs?	**Gümrükte sorun çıkar mı?** gyum•ryuk•_teh_ soh•_roon_ chih•_kahr_ mih
Is there a certificate of authenticity?	**Hakikilik belgesi var mı?** hah•_kee_•kee•leek behl•geh•_see_ _vahr_ mih

Clothing

I'd like…	**…istiyorum.** …ees•_tee_•yoh•room
Can I try this on?	**Bunu deneyebilir miyim?** boo•_noo_ deh•neh•yeh•bee•_leer_ mee•yeem
It doesn't fit.	**Olmadı.** _ohl_•mah•dih

It's too...	**Çok...** _chohk..._
big	**büyük** _byu·yyuk_
small	**küçük** _kyu·chyuk_
short	**kısa** _kih·sah_
long	**uzun** _oo·zoon_
Do you have this in size...?	**Bunun...bedeni var mı?** _boo·noon...beh·deh·nee vahr mih_
Do you have this in a bigger/smaller size?	**Bunun daha büyük/küçük bedeni var mı?** _boo·noon dah·hah byu·yyuk/kyu·chyuk beh·deh·nee vahr mih_

For Numbers, see page 176.

127

YOU MAY SEE...

ERKEK GİYİMİ	men's clothing
BAYAN GİYİMİ	women's clothing
ÇOCUK GİYİMİ	children's clothing

Colors

I'm looking for something in...	**...bir şeyler arıyorum.** _...beer shay·lehr ah·rih·yoh·room_
beige	**Bej** _behj_
black	**Siyah** _see·yah_
blue	**Mavi** _mah·vee_
brown	**Kahverengi** _kah·veh·rehn·gee_
green	**Yeşil** _yeh·sheel_
gray	**Gri** _gree_
orange	**Portakal rengi** _pohr·tah·kahl rehn·gee_
pink	**Pembe** _pehm·beh_
purple	**Mor** _mohr_

red	**Kırmızı** kihr•mih•*zih*
white	**Beyaz** beh•*yahz*
yellow	**Sarı** sah•*rih*

Clothes & Accessories

backpack	**sırt çantası** sihrt chahn•tah•*sih*
belt	**kemer** keh•*mehr*
bikini	**bikini** bee•*kee*•nee
blouse	**bluz** blooz
bra	**sütyen** syut•*yehn*
briefs [underpants]	**külot** kyu•*loht*
coat	**palto** pahl•*toh*
dress	**elbise** ehl•*bee*•seh
hat	**şapka** shahp•*kah*
jacket	**ceket** jeh•*keht*
jeans	**kot pantalon** koht pahn•tah•*lohn*
pajamas	**pijama** pee•*jah*•mah
pants [trousers]	**pantalon** pahn•tah•*lohn*
pantyhose [tights]	**tayt** tiet
purse [handbag]	**el çantası** ehl chahn•tah•*sih*
raincoat	**yağmurluk** *yah*•moor•look
scarf	**eşarp** eh•*shahrp*
shirt (men's)	**gömlek** gurm•*lehk*
shorts	**şort** shohrt
skirt	**etek** eh•*tehk*
socks	**çorap** choh•*rahp*
suit	**takım elbise** tah•kihm ehl•*bee*•seh
sunglasses	**güneş gözlüğü** gyu•*nehsh* gurz•lyu•*yyu*
sweater	**süveter** syu•*veh*•tehr
sweatshirt	**sweatshirt** *sveht*•shurrt

swimming trunks/ swimsuit	**mayo** _mah•yoh_
T-shirt	**tişört** _tee•shurrt_
tie	**kravat** _krah•vaht_
underwear	**külot** _kyu•loht_

Fabric

I'd like…	**…istiyorum.** _. . .ees•tee•yoh•room_
cotton	**Pamuklu** _pah•mook•loo_
denim	**Kot kumaşı** _koht koo•mah•shih_
lace	**Dantel** _dahn•tehl_
leather	**Deri** _deh•ree_
linen	**Keten** _keh•tehn_
silk	**İpek** _ee•pehk_
wool	**Yün** _yyun_
Is it machine washable?	**Makinede yıkanabilir mi?** _mah•kee•neh•deh yih•kah•nah•bee•leer mee_

Shoes

I'd like...	**...istiyorum.** . . . *ees·tee·yoh·room*
high-heeled/ flat shoes	**Yüksek topuklu/Düz taban ayakkabı** *yyuk·sehk toh·pook·loo/dyuz tah·bahn ah·yahk·kah·bih*
boots	**Çizme** *cheez·meh*
loafers	**Mokasen** *moh·kah·sehn*
sandals	**Sandalet** *sahn·dah·leht*
shoes	**Ayakkabı** *ah·yahk·kah·bih*
slippers	**Terlik** *tehr·leek*
sneakers	**Koşu ayakkabısı** *koh·shoo ah·yahk·kah·bih·sih*
In size...	**...numara.** . . . *noo·mah·rah*

For Numbers, see page 176.

Sizes

small	**küçük** *kyu·chyuk*
medium	**orta** *ohr·tah*
large	**büyük** *byu·yyuk*
extra large	**çok büyük** *chohk byu·yyuk*
petite	**ufak** *oo·fahk*
plus size	**battal boy** *baht·tahl boy*

Newsagent & Tobacconist

Do you sell English- language books/ newspapers?	**İngilizce kitap/gazete satıyor musunuz?** *een·gee·leez·jeh kee·tahp/gah·zeh·teh sah·tih·yohr moo·soo·nooz*
I'd like...	**...istiyorum.** . . . *ees·tee·yoh·room*
candy [sweets]	**Şeker** *sheh·kehr*
chewing gum	**Sakız** *sah·kihz*
a chocolate bar	**Çikolata** *chee·koh·lah·tah*
cigars	**Puro** *poo·roh*

a pack/carton of cigarettes	**Paket/Karton sigara** pah·_keht_/cahr·_tohn_ see·gah·_rah_
a lighter	**Çakmak** chahk·_mahk_
a magazine	**Dergi** dehr·_gee_
matches	**Kibrit** keeb·_reet_
a newspaper	**Gazete** gah·_zeh_·teh
a road/town map of…	**…yol/kent haritası** …yohl/kehnt hah·ree·tah·_sih_
stamps	**Pul** pool

You can find many English-language newspapers at newsstands in major cities, at airports and bus and train stations.

Photography

I'm looking for...	**...bir fotoğraf makinesi arıyorum.** ....*beer*
camera.	*foh•toh•<u>rahf</u> mah•<u>kee</u>•neh•see ah•<u>rih</u>•yoh•room*
an automatic	**Otomatik** *oh•toh•mah•<u>teek</u>*
a digital	**Dijital** *dee•jee•<u>tahl</u>*
a disposable	**Tek kullanımlık** *<u>tehk</u> kool•<u>lah</u>•nihm•lihk*
I'd like...	**...istiyorum.** ....*ees•<u>tee</u>•yoh•room*
a battery	**Pil** *peel*
digital prints	**Dijital baskı** *dee•jee•<u>tahl</u> bahs•<u>kih</u>*
a memory card	**Hafıza kartı** *hah•fih•<u>zah</u> kahr•<u>tih</u>*
Can I print digital photos here?	**Dijital fotoğrafları burda basabilir miyim?** *dee•jee•<u>tahl</u> foh•toh•<u>rahf</u>•lah•rih boor•dah bah•sah•bee•<u>leer</u> mee•yeem*

Souvenirs

bottle of wine	**bir şişe şarap** *beer shee•<u>sheh</u> shah•<u>rahp</u>*
box of chocolates	**kutu çikolata** *koo•<u>too</u> chee•koh•<u>lah</u>•tah*
calendar	**takvim** *tahk•<u>veem</u>*
carpets	**halı** *hah•<u>lih</u>*
dolls	**bebek** *beh•<u>behk</u>*
jewelry	**mücevher** *myu•jehv•<u>hehr</u>*

key ring	**anahtarlık** *ah·nahh·tahr·lihk*
lace	**dantel** *dahn·tehl*
leather goods	**deri eşyalar** *deh·ree ehsh·yah·lahr*
perfume	**parfüm** *pahr·fyum*
porcelain	**porselen** *pohr·seh·lehn*
postcards	**kartpostal** *kahrt·pohs·tahl*
pottery	**çömlek** *churm·lehk*
rug	**kilim** *kee·leem*
scarf	**eşarp** *eh·shahrp*
silk garments	**ipek eşya** *ee·pehk ehsh·yah*
souvenir guide	**hediyelik eşya rehberi** *heh·dee·yeh·leek ehsh·yah reh·beh·ree*
T-shirt	**tişört** *tee·shurrt*
tea towel	**kurulama bezi** *koo·roo·lah·mah beh·zee*
Can I see this/that?	**Buna/Şuna bakabilir miyim?** *boo·nah/shoo·nah bah·kah·bee·leer mee·yeem*
It's the one in the window/display case.	**Vitrindeki./Sergilenen.** *veet·reen·deh·kee/sehr·gee·leh·nehn*
I'd like…	**…istiyorum.** *…ees·tee·yoh·room*
a battery	**Pil** *peel*
a bracelet	**Bilezik** *bee·leh·zeek*

133

For everything under one roof, be sure to go shopping in the **Kapali Çarsi** (covered market or Grand Bazaar) in Istanbul. One of the largest covered markets in the world, there are literally thousands of shops and restaurants selling just about anything imaginable. Here you'll be able to find lots of Turkish souvenirs to take back home with you and it's a great chance to practice your haggling skills! Be sure to enjoy the ambiance, but stay alert for pickpockets and bag snatchers.

a brooch	**Broş** *brohsh*
earrings	**Küpe** *kyu·<u>peh</u>*
a necklace	**Kolye** *kohl·<u>yeh</u>*
a ring	**Yüzük** *yyu·<u>zyuk</u>*
a watch	**Kol saati** <u>*kohl*</u> *sah·ah·<u>tee</u>*
copper	**Bakır** *bah·<u>kihr</u>*
crystal	**Kuartz** *koo·<u>ahrtz</u>*
diamond	**Elmas** *ehl·<u>mahs</u>*
white/yellow gold	**Beyaz/Sarı altın** *beh·<u>yahz</u>/sah·<u>rih</u> ahl·<u>tihn</u>*
pearl	**İnci** *een·<u>jee</u>*
pewter	**Kurşun-kalay alaşımı** *koor·<u>shoon</u> kah·<u>lie</u> ah·lah·shih·<u>mih</u>*
platinum	**Platin** *plah·<u>teen</u>*
sterling silver	**Som gümüş** *sohm gyu·<u>myush</u>*
Is this real?	**Hakiki mi?** *hah·kee·<u>kee</u> mee*
Can you engrave it?	**İşleyebilir misin?** *eesh·leh·yeh·bee·<u>leer</u> mee·seen*

ESSENTIAL

When's the game?	**Maç kaçta?**	mahch kahch·tah
Where's…?	**…nerede?**	…neh·reh·deh
the beach	**Plaj**	plahj
the park	**Park**	pahrk
the pool	**Yüzme havuzu**	yyuz·meh hah·voo·zoo
Is it safe to swim/ dive here?	**Burada yüzmek/dalmak güvenli mi?**	boo·rah·dah yyuz·mehk/dahl·mahk gyu·vehn·lee mee
Can I rent [hire] golf clubs?	**Golf sopalarını kiralayabilir miyim?**	gohlf soh·pah·lah·rih·nih kee·rah·lah·yah·bee·leer mee·yeem
How much per hour?	**Saatlik ücreti nedir?**	sah·aht·leek yuj·reh·tee neh·deer
How far is it to…?	**…buradan ne kadar uzakta?**	…boo·rah·dahn neh kah·dahr oo·zahk·tah
Can you show me on the map?	**Bana haritada gösterebilir misiniz?**	bah·nah hah·ree·tah·dah gurs·teh·reh·bee·leer mee·see·neez

Watching Sport

When's…?	**…ne zaman?**	…neh zah·mahn
the basketball game	**Basketbol maçı**	bahs·keht·bohl mah·chih
the boxing match	**Boks maçı**	bohks mah·chih
the cycling race	**Bisiklet yarışı**	bee·seek·leht yah·rih·shih
the golf tournament	**Golf turnuvası**	gohlf toor·noo·vah·sih
the soccer game	**Futbol maçı**	foot·bohl mah·chih

the tennis match	**Tenis maçı** *teh·nees mah·chih*
the volleyball game	**Voleybol maçı** *voh·lay·bohl mah·chih*
Which teams are playing?	**Hangi takımlar oynuyor?** *hahn·gee tah·kihm·lahr oy·noo·yohr*
Where's…?	**…nerede?** *…neh·reh·deh*
the horsetrack	**At yarışı** *aht yah·rih·shih*
the racetrack	**Hipodrom** *hee·pohd·rohm*
the stadium	**Stadyum** *stah·dyoom*
Where can I place a bet?	**Nerede bahis oynayabilirim?** *neh·reh·deh bah·hees oy·nah·yah·bee·lee·reem*

For Tickets, see page 19.

Playing Sport

Where's…?	**…nerede?** *…neh·reh·deh*
the golf course	**Golf sahası** *gohlf sah·hah·sih*
the gym	**Spor klübü** *spohr klyu·byu*
the park	**Park** *pahrk*
the tennis courts	**Tenis kortları** *teh·nees kohrt·lah·rih*
How much per…?	**…ücreti nedir?** *…yuj·reh·tee neh·deer*
day	**Günlük** *gyun·lyuk*

Since Turkey is surrounded by so much water, it is no surprise that water sports are popular. Swimming, sailing, scuba diving and windsurfing are common in the seas, while one can go rafting or canoeing on one of Turkey's many rivers. Other sports like caving and trekking can be enjoyed in addition to golf or horseback riding. The national sports, however, are soccer and wrestling. Oil wrestling has in fact been practiced since Ottoman times.

hour	**Saatlik** *sah•aht•<u>leek</u>*
game	**Bir oyun** *beer oh•<u>yoon</u>*
round	**Bir tur** *beer toor*
Can I rent [hire]…?	**…kiralayabilir miyim?**
	…kee•rah•lah•yah•bee•<u>leer</u> mee•yeem
golf clubs	**Sopa** *soh•<u>pah</u>*
equipment	**Donanım** *doh•nah•<u>nihm</u>*
a racket	**Raket** *rah•<u>keht</u>*

At the Beach/Pool

Where's the beach/pool?	**Plaj/Havuz nerede?** *plahj/hah•<u>vooz</u> <u>neh</u>•reh•deh*
Is there…?	**Burada…var mı?** *<u>boo</u>•rah•dah…<u>vahr</u> mih*
a kiddie [paddling] pool	**çocuk havuzu** *choh•<u>jook</u> hah•voo•zoo*
an indoor/outdoor pool	**kapalı/açık havuz** *kah•pah•<u>lih</u>/ah•<u>chihk</u> hah•<u>vooz</u>*
a lifeguard	**cankurtaran** *jan•<u>koor</u>•tah•rahn*
Is it safe…?	**…güvenli mi?** *…gyu•vehn•<u>lee</u> mee*
to swim	**Yüzmek** *yyuz•<u>mehk</u>*

to dive	**Dalmak** *dahl•mahk*
for children	**Çocuklar için** *choh•jook•lahr ee•cheen*
I want to rent [hire]...	**...Kiralamak istiyorum.** *...kee•rah•lah•mahk ees•tee•yoh•room*
a deck chair	**Katlanabilir koltuk** *kaht•lah•nah•bee•leer kohl•took*
diving equipment	**Dalış donanımı** *dah•lihsh doh•nah•nih•mih*
a jet-ski	**Jet ski** *jeht skee*
a motorboat	**Deniz motoru** *deh•neez moh•toh•roo*
a rowboat	**Sandal** *sahn•dahl*
snorkeling equipment	**Şnorkel takımı** *shnohr•kehl tah•kih•mih*

YOU MAY SEE...

ÇEKİCİ TELEFERİK	drag lift
TELEFERİK	cable car
KOLTUKLU TELEFERİK	chair lift
Acemi	novice
Orta seviyede	intermediate
Uzman	expert
Pist kapalı	trail [piste] closed

a surfboard	**Surf tahtası** *surrf tah·htah·sih*
a towel	**Havlu** *hahv·loo*
an umbrella	**Şemsiye** *shehm·see·ih*
water skis	**Su kayağı** *soo kah·yah·ih*
windsurfer	**Rüzgar sörfçüsü** *ryuz·gahr surrf·chyu·syu*

Though most people associate Turkey with a hot climate, Turkey is actually quite mountainous and there is very good skiing to be enjoyed throughout the country. The following is a list of the major ski resorts and their locations: Ankara – Elmadag, outside of Ankara; Antalya – Saklikent, northwest of Antalya; Bolu-Kartalkaya, off the Istanbul – Ankara highway; Bursa – Uludag, just south of Bursa; Erzurum-Palandoken, near Erzurum; Ilgaz Dagi, between Kastamonu and Cankiri; Kars – Sarikamis, close to Kars; Kayseri – Erciyes, near Kayseri and Zigana – Gumushane, just outside of Gumushane.

Winter Sports

A lift pass for a day/ five days, please.	**Bir/Beş günlük teleferik pasosu lütfen.** *beer/ behsh gyun·lyuk teh·leh·feh·reek pah·soh·soo lyut·fehn*
I want to rent [hire]...	**...kiralamak istiyorum.** *...kee·rah·lah·mahk ees·tee·yoh·room*
boots	**Kayak çizmesi** *kah·yahk cheez·meh·see*
a helmet	**Kask** *kahsk*
poles	**Kayak sopası** *kah·yahk soh·pah·sih*
skis	**Kayak** *kah·yahk*
a snowboard	**Kar kayağı** *kahr kah·yah·ih*
snowshoes	**Kar ayakkabısı** *kahr ah·yahk·kah·bih·sih*

These are too big/small.	**Bunlar çok büyük/küçük.** *boon·lahr chohk byu·yyuk/kyu·chyuk*	
Are there lessons?	**Ders var mı?** *dehrs vahr mih*	
I'm a beginner.	**Yeni başlıyorum.** *yeh·nee bahsh·lih·yoh·room*	
I'm experienced.	**Deneyimliyim.** *deh·neh·yeem·lee·yeem*	
A trail [piste] map, please.	**Pist haritası lütfen.** *peest hah·ree·tah·sih lyut·fehn*	

Out in the Country

I'd like a map of…	**…haritası istiyorum.** *…hah·ree·tah·sih ees·tee·yoh·room*
this region	**Bu bölge** *boo burl·geh*
walking routes	**Yürüyüş yolları** *yyu·ryu·yyush yohl·lah·rih*
bike routes	**Bisiklet yolları** *bee·see·kleht yohl·lah·rih*
the trails	**Dar yollar** *dahr yohl·lahr*
Is it easy?	**Kolay mı?** *koh·lie mih*
Is it difficult?	**Zor mu?** *zohr moo*
Is it far?	**Uzak mı?** *oo·zahk mih*
Is it steep?	**Dik mi?** *deek mee*
How far is it to…?	**…ne kadar uzakta?** *…neh kah·dahr oo·zahk·tah*

Can you show me on the map?	**Bana haritada gösterebilir misiniz?** _bah·nah hah·ree·tah·dah gurs·teh·reh·bee·leer mee·see·neez_
I'm lost.	**Kayboldum.** _kie·bohl·doom_
Where's…?	**…nerede?** _… neh·reh·deh_
the bridge	**Köprü** _kurp·ryu_
the cave	**Mağara** _mah·ah·rah_
the cliff	**Uçurum** _oo·choo·room_
the desert	**Çöl** _churl_
the farm	**Çiftlik** _cheeft·leek_
the field	**Tarla** _tahr·lah_
the forest	**Orman** _ohr·mahn_
the hill	**Tepe** _teh·peh_
the lake	**Göl** _gurl_
the mountain	**Dağ** _dah_
the nature preserve	**Milli park** _meel·lee pahrk_
the overlook	**Hakim tepe** _hah·keem teh·peh_
the park	**Park** _pahrk_
the path	**Patika** _pah·tee·kah_
the peak	**Tepe** _teh·peh_
the picnic area	**Piknik alanı** _peek·neek ah·lah·nih_
the pond	**Gölcük** _gurl·jyuk_
the river	**Irmak** _ihr·mahk_
the sea	**Deniz** _deh·neez_
the thermal springs	**Termal kaynaklar** _tehr·mahl kie·nahk·lahr_
the stream	**Dere** _deh·reh_
the valley	**Vadi** _vah·dee_
the vineyard/winery	**Bağ/Şaraphane** _bah/shah·rahp·hah·neh_
the waterfall	**Şelale** _sheh·lah·leh_

Going Out

ESSENTIAL

What is there to do in the evenings?	**Geceleri ne yapılır?** geh·jeh·leh·ree neh yah·pih·lihr
Do you have a program of events?	**Bir rehberiniz var mı?** beer reh·beh·ree·neez vahr mih
What's playing at the movies [cinema] tonight?	**Bu gece hangi filmler oynuyor?** boo geh·jeh hahn·gee feelm·lehr oy·noo·yohr
Where's…?	**…nerede?** …neh·reh·deh
the downtown area	**Kent merkezi** kehnt mehr·keh·zee
the bar	**Bar** bahr
the dance club	**Diskotek** dees·koh·tehk
Is there a cover charge?	**Giriş ücretli mi?** gee·reesh yuj·reht·lee mee

Entertainment

Can you recommend…?	**…önerebilir misiniz?** …ur·neh·reh·bee·_leer_ mee·see·neez
a concert	**Konser** kohn·_sehr_
a movie	**Film** feelm
an opera	**Opera** oh·_peh_·rah
a play	**Tiyatro oyunu** tee·_yaht_·roh oh·_yoo_·noo
When does it start/end?	**Ne zaman başlıyor/bitiyor?** _neh_ zah·_mahn_ bahsh·_lih_·yohr/bee·_tee_·yohr
What's the dress code?	**Giyim tarzı ne?** gee·_yeem_ tahr·_zih_ neh
I like…	**…severim.** …seh·_veh_·reem
classical music	**Klasik müzik** klah·_seek_ myu·_zeek_
folk music	**Halk müziği** _hahlk_ myu·zee·_yee_
jazz	**Caz** jahz
pop music	**Pop** pohp
rap	**Rep** rehp

For Tickets, see page 19.

Culturally, Turkey has a lot to offer. There are numerous archeological sites spread throughout the country, which represent many different periods in history. The ruins at Efes (Ephesus), for example, are certainly worth a trip. Though the area was inhabited over 6000 years ago, during the Neolithic period, and traces have been excavated from various periods since then, the well-conserved ruins you can visit today are mainly from Roman times, that is, they are more than 2000 years old.

Moreover, there is no shortage of theaters, operas, concert halls and museums, particularly in the larger cities. And many cities in Turkey are host to excellent music, film and dance festivals throughout the year. Visit the local **Turizm Danışma Bürosu** (tourist information offices) to find out what's going on while you are in town.

Nightlife

What is there to do in the evenings?	**Geceleri ne yapılır?** geh·jeh·leh·_ree_ _neh_ _yah_·pih·lihr
Can you recommend…?	**…önerebilir misiniz?** …ur·neh·reh·bee·_leer_ mee·see·neez
a bar	**Bar** bahr
a casino	**Kumarhane** koo·mahr·hah·_neh_
a dance club	**Diskotek** _dees_·koh·tehk
a gay club	**Eşcinsel klübü** _ehsh_·jeen·sehl klyu·_byu_
a nightclub	**Gece klübü** geh·_jeh_ klyu·_byu_
Is there live music?	**Orada canlı müzik var mı?** _oh_·rah·dah _jahn_·lih myu·_zeek_ vahr mih
How do I get there?	**Oraya nasıl gidebilirim?** _oh_·rah·yah nah·sihl gee·deh·bee·lee·reem
Is there a cover charge?	**Masa ücreti var mı?** mah·_sah_ yuj·reh·tee _vahr_ mih
Let's go dancing.	**Hadi dans etmeye gidelim.** hah·_dee_ _dans_ eht·meh·yeh gee·deh·_leem_
Is this area safe at night?	**Bu bölge gece güvenli midir?** boo burl·geh geh·jeh gyu·vehn·lih mih·deer

Special Requirements

Business Travel

ESSENTIAL

I'm here on business.	**İş için burdayım.** _eesh_ ee•cheen boor•_dah_•yihm
Here's my business card.	**Buyrun kartvizitim.** _booy_•roon kahrt•vee•zee•_teem_
Can I have your card?	**Kartınızı alabilirmiyim?** kahr•tih•nih•_zih_ ah•lah•bee•_leer_ mee•yeem
I have a meeting with...	**...ile bir randevum var.** ...ee•_leh_ beer rahn•deh•_voom_ vahr
Where's...?	**...nerede?** ..._neh_•reh•deh
the business center	**İş merkezi** _eesh_ mehr•keh•zee
the convention hall	**Kongre salonu** kohng•_reh_ sah•loh•_noo_
the meeting room	**Toplantı odası** tohp•_lahn_•tih oh•_dah_•sih

On Business

I'm here to attend...	**...katılmak için burdayım.** ...kah•_tihl_•mahk ee•cheen boor•_dah_•yihm
a seminar	**Seminere** seh•_mee_•nehr
a conference	**Konferansa** kohn•feh•_rahn_•sah
a meeting	**Toplantıya** tohp•lahn•tih•_yah_
My name is...	**İsmim...** ees•_meem_...
May I introduce my colleague...?	**...meslektaşımı tanıtabilir miyim?** ...mehs•lehk•_tah_•shih•mih tah•nih•tah•bee•_leer_ mee•yeem
I have a meeting/an appointment with...	**...ile bir toplantım/randevum var.** ...ee•_leh_ beer tohp•lahn•_tihm_/rahn•deh•_voom_ vahr
I'm sorry I'm late.	**Üzgünüm, geciktim.** yuz•_gyu_•nyum geh•jeek•_teem_

When people meet in a professional setting, generally they shake hands and say **merhaba** (hello). Drinking small cups of tea throughout the day is a common practice in places of business, and visitors are likely to be offered tea as well. Note that some traditional people avoid shaking hands with people they are meeting for the first time. If so, this will be evident in their behavior (not offering a hand, staying several feet away). In such circumstances, an exchange of verbal greetings, eye contact and smiles should suffice.

I need an interpreter.	**Tercüman istiyorum.** *tehr·jyu·mahn ees·tee·yoh·room*	
You can reach me at the…Hotel.	**…otelden bana ulaşabilirsin.** …*oh·tehl·dehn bah·nah oo·lah·shah·bee·leer·seen*	
I'm here until…	**…kadar burdayım.** …*kah·dahr boor·dah·yihm*	
I need to…	**…gerek.** …*yahp·mahm geh·rehk*	
make a call	**Telefon görüşmesi yapmam** *teh·leh·fohn gur·ryush·meh·see*	
make a photocopy	**Bir fotokopi yapmam** *beer foh·toh·koh·pee*	
send an e-mail	**E-posta göndermem** *eh·pohs·tah gurn·dehr·mehm*	

send a fax	**Faks çekmem** _fahks_ **chehk•**_mehm_
send a package	**Paket göndermem** _pah•_keht_ gurn•dehr•_mehm_
It was a pleasure to meet you.	**Sizinle tanışmaktan memnun oldum.** _see•_zeen_•leh tah•nihsh•mahk•_tahn_ mehm•_noon_ ohl•doom_

For Communications, see page 53.

For Communications, see page 53.

YOU MAY HEAR...

Randevunuz mu var? _rahn•deh•voo•_nooz_ moo vahr_	Do you have an appointment?
Kiminle? _kee•_meen_•leh_	With whom?
O toplantıda. _oh tohp•lahn•tih•_dah_	He/She is in a meeting.
Bir dakika lütfen. _beer dah•_kee_•kah _lyut_•fehn_	One moment, please.
Oturun. _oh•_too_•roon_	Have a seat.
İçecek birşeyler istermisiniz? _ee•cheh•_jehk_ beer shay•_lehr_ ees•_tehr_•mee•see•neez_	Would you like something to drink?
Geldiğiniz için teşekkürler. _gehl•dee•ee•_neez_ ee•cheen teh•shehk•kyur•_lehr_	Thank you for coming.

Traveling with Children

ESSENTIAL

Is there a discount for children?	**Çocuklar için indirim var mı?** choh•jook•_lahr_ ee•_cheen_ een•dee•_reem_ vahr mih
Can you recommend a babysitter?	**Bir çocuk bakıcısı önerebilir misiniz?** beer choh•_jook_ bah•kih•jih•_sih_ ur•neh•reh•bee•_leer_ mee•see•neez
Could we have a child's seat/highchair?	**Çocuk sandalyesi/Yüksek sandalye alabilir miyiz?** choh•_jook_ sahn•dahl•yeh•_see_/yyuk•_sehk_ sahn•dahl•_yeh_ ah•lah•bee•_leer_ mee•yeez
Where can I change the baby?	**Bebeğin altını nerede değiştirebilirim?** beh•beh•_yeen_ ahl•tih•_nih_ neh•reh•deh deh•yecsh•tee•reh•bee•_lee_•reem

Out & About

Can you recommend something for the kids?	**Çocuklar için birşeyler önerir misiniz?** choh•jook•_lahr_ ee•_cheen_ beer shay•lehr ur•neh•_reer_ mee•see•neez
Where's…?	**…nerede?** … neh•reh•deh
the amusement park	**Oyun parkı** oh•_yoon_ pahr•_kih_
the arcade	**Oyun salonu** oh•_yoon_ sah•loh•_noo_
the kiddie [paddling] pool	**Çocuk havuzu** choh•_jook_ hah•voo•_zoo_
the park	**Park** pahrk
the playground	**Çocuk parkı** choh•_jook_ pahr•_kih_
the zoo	**Hayvanat bahçesi** hie•vah•_naht_ bah•cheh•_see_

Are kids allowed?	**Çocuklara serbest mi?** _choh•jook•lah•rah_ sehr•_behst_ mee
Is it safe for kids?	**Çocuklar için güvenli mi?** _choh•jook_•lahr ee•cheen gyu•_vehn_•lee mee
Is it suitable for... year olds?	**...yaş için uygun mu?** ..._yash_ ee•cheen ooy•_goon_ moo

For Numbers, see page 176.

YOU MAY HEAR...

You May Hear...

Ne kadar sevimli! _neh_ kah•dahr seh•veem•lee How cute!
İsmi ne? ees•_mee neh_ What's his/her name?
Kaç yaşında? _kach_ yah•shihn•dah How old is he/she?

Baby Essentials

Do you have...?	**...var mı?** ..._vahr_ mih
a baby bottle	**Biberon** bee•beh•_rohn_
baby wipes	**Bebek mendili** beh•_behk_ mehn•dee•_lee_

a car seat	**Araba koltuğu** *ah·rah·bah kohl·too·oo*
a children's menu/ portion	**Çocuk menüsü/porsiyonu** *choh·jook meh·nyu·syu/ pohr·see·yoh·noo*
a child's seat	**Çocuk sandalyesi** *choh·jook sahn·dahl·yeh·see*
a cot	**Çocuk Beşik** *choh·jook beh·sheek*
a crib	**Çocuk yatağı** *choh·jook yah·tah·ih*
diapers [nappies]	**Bebek bezi** *beh·bek beh·zee*
formula	**Formül** *fohr·myul*
a highchair	**Çocuk Yüksek sandalye** *choh·jook yyuk·sehk sahn·dahl·yeh*
a pacifier [dummy]	**Yatıştırıcı** *yah·tihsh·tih·rih·jih*
a playpen	**Portatif çocuk** *parkı pohr·tah·teef choh·jook pahr·kih*
a stroller [push chair]	**Puset** *poo·seht*
Can I breastfeed the baby here?	**Bebeği burda emzirebilir miyim?** *beh·beh·yee boor·dah ehm·zee·reh·bee·leer mee·yeem*
Where can I change the baby?	**Bebeğin altını nerede değiştirebilirim?** *beh·beh·yeen ahl·tih·nih neh·reh·deh deh·yeesh·tee·reh·bee·lee·reem*

For Dining with Children, see page 70.

Babysitting

Can you recommend a babysitter?	**Bir çocuk bakıcısı önerebilir misiniz?** *beer choh-jook bah-kih-jih-sih ur-neh-reh-bee-leer mee-see-neez*
What's the charge?	**Ücreti nedir?** *yuj-reh-tee neh-deer*
We'll be back by...	**...kadar geri döneriz.** ...*kah-dahr geh-ree dur-neh-reez*
I can be reached at...	**Bana...ulaşabilirsiniz.** *bah-nah... oo-lah-shah-bee-leer-see-neez*

For Numbers, see page 176.

Health & Emergency

Can you recommend a pediatrician?	**Bir çocuk doktoru önerir misiniz?** *beer choh-jook dohk-toh-roo ur-neh-reer mee-see-neez*
My child is allergic to...	**Çocuğumun...alerjisi var.** *choh-joo-oo-moon... ah-lehr-jee-see vahr*
My child is missing.	**Çocuğum kayıp.** *choh-joo-oom kah-yihp*
Have you seen a boy/girl?	**Bir oğlan/kız gördünüz mü?** *beer oo-lahn/kihz gurr-dyu-nyuz myu*

For Meals & Cooking, see page 73.

For Health, see page 160.

For Police, see page 158.

Disabled Travelers

ESSENTIAL

Is there…?	**…var mı?** … *vahr mih*
access for the disabled	**Engelli girişi** *ehn·gehl·lee gee·ree·shee*
a wheelchair ramp	**Tekerlekli sandalye rampası** *teh·kehr·lehk·lee sahn·dahl·yeh rahm·pah·sih*
a handicapped [disabled-] accessible restroom [toilet]	**Özürlü tuvaleti** *ur·zyur·lyu too·vah·leh·tee*
I need…	**…ihtiyacım var.** … *eeh·tee·yah·jihm vahr*
assistance	**Yardımcıya** *yahr·dihm·jih·yah*
an elevator [lift]	**Asansöre** *ah·sahn·sur·reh*
a ground-floor room	**Zemin-kat odasına** *zeh·meen·kaht oh·dah·sih·nah*

Asking for Assistance

I'm disabled.	**Ben özürlüyüm.** *behn ur·zyur·lyu·yyum*
I'm deaf.	**Ben sağırım.** *behn sah·ih·rihm*
I'm visually/hearing impaired.	**Görme/Duyma engelliyim.** *gurr·meh/dooy·mah ehn·gel·lee·yeem*
I'm unable to walk far.	**Uzağa yürüyemem.** *oo·zah·ah yyu·ryu·yeh·mehm*
I'm unable to use the stairs.	**Merdivenleri kullanamam.** *mehr·dee·vehn·leh·ree kool·lah·nah·mahm*
Can I bring my wheelchair?	**Tekerlekli sandalyemi getirebilir miyim?** *teh·kehr·lehk·lee sahn·dahl·yeh·mee geh·tee·reh·bee·leer mee·yeem*
Are guide dogs permitted?	**Rehber köpeklere izin var mı?** *reh·behr kur·pehk·leh·reh ee·zeen vahr mih*
Can you help me?	**Bana yardım edebilir misiniz?** *bah·nah yahr·dihm eh·deh·bee·leer mee·see·neez*
Please open/hold the door.	**Lütfen kapıyı açın/tutun.** *lyut·fehn kah·pih·yih ah·chihn/too·toon*

In an
Emergency

Emergencies

ESSENTIAL

Help!	**İmdat!**	*eem-<u>daht</u>*
Go away!	**Çekil git!**	*cheh-<u>keel</u> geet*
Stop thief!	**Durdurun, hırsız!**	*door-<u>doo</u>-roon hihr-<u>sihz</u>*
Get a doctor!	**Bir doktor bulun!**	*beer dohk-<u>tohr</u> boo-loon*
Fire!	**Yangın!**	*yahn-<u>gihn</u>*
I'm lost.	**Kayboldum.**	*<u>kie</u>-bohl-doom*
Can you help me?	**Bana yardım edebilir misiniz?**	*bah-nah yahr-<u>dihm</u> eh-deh-bee-<u>leer</u> mee-see-neez*

YOU MAY HEAR...

Bu formu doldurun lütfen. *boo <u>fohr</u>-moo dohl-<u>doo</u>-roon <u>lyut</u>-fehn*	Please fill out this form.
Kimliğiniz lütfen. *keem-lee-yee-<u>neez</u> <u>lyut</u>-fehn*	Your identification, please.
Ne zaman/Nerede oldu? *<u>neh</u> zah-mahn/ <u>neh</u>-reh-deh ohl-doo*	When/Where did it happen?
Nasıl biriydi? *<u>nah</u>-sihl bee-<u>reey</u>-dee*	What did he/she look like?

Police

ESSENTIAL

Call the police!	**Polis çağırın!** poh‑_lees_ _chah_‑ih‑rihn
Where's the police station?	**Karakol nerede?** kah‑rah‑_kohl_ _neh_‑reh‑deh
There has been an accident/attack.	**Bir kaza/saldırı oldu.** beer kah‑_zah_/sahl‑_dih_‑rih ohl‑doo
My child is missing.	**Çocuğum kayıp.** choh‑joo‑_oom_ kah‑_yihp_
I need…	**…ihtiyacım var.** …eeh‑tee‑yah‑_jihm_ vahr
an interpreter	**Tercümana** tehr‑jyu‑mah‑_nah_
to contact my lawyer	**Avukatımla görüşmeye** ah‑voo‑kah‑_tihm_‑lah _gur_‑ryush‑meh‑_yeh_
to make a phone call	**Telefon görüşmesi yapmaya** teh‑leh‑_fohn_ gur‑ryush‑meh‑_see_ yahp‑mah‑_yah_
I'm innocent.	**Masumum.** mah‑_soo_‑moom

Crime & Lost Property

I want to report…	**Bir…haber vermek istiyorum.** beer…hah‑_behr_ vehr‑mehk ees‑_tee_‑yoh‑room
a mugging	**gasp** gahsp
a rape	**tecavüz** teh‑jah‑_vyuz_
a theft	**hırsızlık** hihr‑sihz‑_lihk_
I've been robbed/ mugged.	**Çarpıldım/Soyuldum.** chah‑rpihl‑dihm/ soh‑yool‑_doom_
I've lost my…	**…kaybettim.** …_kie_‑beht‑teem

My...has been stolen.	**...çalındı.**	*...chah·lihn·dih*
backpack	**Sırt çantam**	*sihrt chahn·tahm*
bicycle	**Bisikletim**	*bee·seek·leh·teem*
camera	**Fotoğraf makinem**	*foh·toh·rahf mah·kee·nehm*
(rental) car	**(Kiralık) Arabam**	*(kee·rah·lihk) ah·rah·bahm*
computer	**Bilgisayarım**	*beel·gee·sah·yah·rihm*
credit card	**Kredi kartlarım**	*kreh·dee kahrt·lah·rihm*
jewelry	**Mücevheratım**	*myu·jehv·heh·rah·tihm*
money	**Param**	*pah·rahm*
passport	**Pasaportum**	*pah·sah·pohr·toom*
purse [handbag]	**Cüzdanım**	*jyuz·dah·nihm*
traveler's checks [cheques]	**Seyahat çeklerim**	*seh·yah·haht chehk·leh·reem*
wallet	**Cüzdanım**	*jyuz·dah·nihm*
I need a police report.	**Polis raporuna ihtiyacım var.**	*poh·lees rah·poh·rooh·nah eeh·tee·yah·jihm vahr*
Where is the British/ American/Irish embassy?	**İngiliz/Amerikan/İrlanda büyükelçiliği nerede?**	*een·geeh·leez/ah·meh·rih·kahn/ ehr·lahn·dah byu·yuhk·ehl·chee·lih·ee neh·reh·deh*

Health

ESSENTIAL

I'm sick [ill].	**Hastayım.** hahs•_tah_•yihm
I need an English-speaking doctor.	**İngilizce konuşan bir doktora ihtiyacım var.** een•gee•_leez_•jeh koh•noo•_shahn_ beer dohk•toh•_rah_ eeh•tee•yah•_jihm_ vahr
It hurts here.	**Burası acıyor.** _boo_•rah•sih ah•_jih_•yohr
I have a stomachache.	**Mide ağrım var.** mee•deh **ah**•rihm vahr

Finding a Doctor

Can you recommend a doctor/dentist?	**Bir doktor/dişçi önerir misiniz?** beer dohk•_tohr_/ _deesh_•chee ur•neh•_reer_ mee•see•neez
Could the doctor come to see me here?	**Doktor beni gelip burada görebilir mi?** dohk•_tohr_ beh•_nee_ geh•_leep_ boo•rah•dah gur•reh•bee•_leer_ mee
I need an English-speaking doctor.	**İngilizce konuşan bir doktora ihtiyacım var.** een•gee•_leez_•jeh koh•noo•_shahn_ beer dohk•toh•_rah_ eeh•tee•yah•_jihm_ vahr

What are the office hours?	**Çalışma saatleri nedir?** *chah·lihsh·mah sah·aht·leh·ree neh·deer*
Can I make an appointment...?	**...için randevu alabilir miyim?** *...ee·cheen rahn·deh·voo ah·lah·bee·leer mee·yeem*
for today	**Bugün** *boo·gyun*
for tomorrow	**Yarın** *yah·rihn*
as soon as possible	**En yakın zaman** *ehn yah·kihn zah·mahn*
It's urgent.	**Acil.** *ah·jeel*

161

Symptoms

I'm bleeding.	**Kanamam var.** *kah·nah·mahm vahr*
I'm constipated.	**Kabızım.** *kah·bih·zihm*
I'm dizzy.	**Başım dönüyor.** *bah·shihm dur·nyu·yohr*
I'm nauseous/vomiting.	**Bulantım var./Kusuyorum.** *boo·lahn·tihm vahr/ koo·soo·yoh·room*
It hurts here.	**Burası acıyor.** *boo·rah·sih ah·jih·yohr*
I have...	**...var.** *...vahr*
an allergic reaction	**Alerjik reaksiyonum** *ah·lehr·jeek reh·ahk·see·yoh·noom*
chest pain	**Göğüs ağrım** *gur·yus ah·rihm*
an earache	**Kulak ağrım** *koo·lahk ah·rihm*
a fever	**Ateşim** *ah·teh·sheem*
pain	**Ağrım** *ah·rihm*
a rash	**Kaşıntım** *kah·shihn·tihm*
a sprain	**Burkulmam** *boor·kool·mahm*
some swelling	**Şişliğim** *sheesh·lee·eem*
a stomachache	**Mide ağrım** *mee·deh ah·rihm*
sunstroke	**Güneş çarpmam** *gyu·nehsh chahrp·mahm*
I've been sick [ill] for...days.	**...gündür hastayım.** *...gyun·dyur hahs·tah·yihm*

For Numbers, see page 176.

Conditions

I'm...	**Ben...** *ben*
anemic	**anemi hastasıyım** *ah•neh•mee hahs•tah•sih•yihm*
asthmatic	**astım** *ahs•tihm*
diabetic	**şeker hastasıyım** *sheh•kehr hahs•tah•sih•yihm*
epileptic	**sara hastasıyım** *sah•rah has•tah•sih•yihm*
I'm allergic to antibiotics/penicillin.	**Antibiyotiğe/Penisiline alerjim var.** *ahn•tee•bee•yoh•tee•yeh/peh•nee•see•lee•neh ah•lehr•jeem vahr*
I have arthritis.	**Artiritim.** *ahr•tee•ree•teem*
I have (high/low) blood pressure.	**(Yüksek/Düşük) Tansiyonum var.** *(yyuk•sehk/dyu•shyuk) tahn•see•yoh•noom vahr*
I have a heart condition.	**Kalbimden rahatsızım.** *kahl•beem•dehn rah•hat•sih•zihm*
I'm on...	**...dayım.** *...dah•yihm*

Treatment

Do I need a prescription/ medicine?	**Reçeteye/ilaca ihtiyacım var mı?** *reh•cheh•teh•yeh/ee•lah•jah eeh•tee•yah•jihm vahr mih?*

| Can you prescribe a generic drug? [unbranded medication]? | **Genel bir ilaç yazabilir misiniz?** geh•nehl beer ee•lahch yah•zah•bee•leer mee•see•neez? |
| Where can I get it? | **Nereden alabilirim?** neh•reh•den ah•lah•bee•lee•reem? |

For Pharmacy, see page 166.

YOU MAY HEAR...

Sorununuz ne? soh•roo•noo•nooz neh	What's wrong?
Neresi acıyor? neh•reh•see ah•jih•yohr	Where does it hurt?
Burası acıyor mu? boo•rah•sih ah•jih•yohr moo	Does it hurt here?
Başka ilaç alıyor musunuz? bahsh•kah ee•lahch ah•lih•yohr moo•soo•nooz	Are you taking any other medication?
Herhangi bir şeye alerjiniz var mı? hehr•hahn•gee beer sheh•yeh ah•lehr•jee•neez vahr mih	Are you allergic to anything?
Ağzınızı açın. ah•zih•nih•zih ah•chihn	Open your mouth.
Derin nefes alın. deh•reen neh•fes ah•lihn	Breathe deeply.
Hastaneye gitmenizi istiyorum. hahs•tah•neh•yeh geet•meh•nee•zee ees•tee•yoh•room	I want you to go to the hospital.

Hospital

| Please notify my family. | **Lütfen aileme bildirin.** lyut•fehn ah•ee•leh•meh beel•dee•reen |
| I'm in pain. | **Acı içindeyim.** ah•jih ee•cheen•deh•yeem |

I need a doctor/nurse.	**Doktora/Hemşireye ihtiyacım var.** *dohk·toh·rah/ hehm·shee·reh·yeh eeh·tee·yah·jihm vahr*
When are visiting hours?	**Ziyaret saatleri ne zaman?** *zee·yah·reht sah·aht·leh·ree neh zah·mahn*
I'm visiting…	**…ziyaret edeceğim.** *…zee·yah·reht eh·deh·jeh·yeem*

Dentist

I've broken a tooth/ lost a filling.	**Dişim kırıldı./Dolgumu düşürdüm.** *dee·sheem kih·rihl·dih/dohl·goo·moo dyu·shyur·dyum*
I have a toothache.	**Dişim ağrıyor.** *dee·sheem ah·rih·yohr*
Can you fix this denture?	**Bu protezi onarabilir misiniz?** *boo proh·teh·zee oh·nah·rah·bee·leer mee·see·neez*

Gynecologist

I have menstrual cramps.	**Aybaşı ağrım.** *ie·bah·shih ah·rihm*
I have a vaginal infection.	**Vajina iltihaplanması var.** *vah·jee·nah eel·tee·hahp·lahn·mah·sih vahr*
I missed my period.	**Günüm gecikti.** *gyu·nyum geh·jeek·tee*
I'm on the Pill.	**Doğum kontrol hapı kullanıyorum.** *doh·oom kohnt·rohl hah·pih kool·lah·nih·yoh·room*

I'm not pregnant.	**Hamile değilim.**	*hah•mee•leh deh•<u>yee</u>•leem*
I'm … months pregnant.	**…aylık hamileyim**	*…ahy•lihk hah•mee•leh•yeem*
I haven't had my period for…months.	**…aydan beri aybaşım olmuyor.**	*…ie•<u>dahn</u> beh•<u>ree</u> ie•bah•<u>shihm</u> ohl•moo•yohr*

For Numbers, see page 176.

Optician

I've lost…	**…kaybettim.**	*…<u>kie</u>•beht•teem*
a contact lens	**Bir kontak lensimi beer**	*kohn•<u>tahk</u> lehn•see•<u>mee</u>*
my glasses	**Gözlüğümü**	*gurz•lyu•yu•<u>myu</u>*
a lens	**Camımı**	*jah•mih•<u>mih</u>*

Payment & Insurance

How much?	**Ne kadar?**	*<u>neh</u> kah•dahr*
Can I pay by credit card?	**Bu kredi kartı ile ödeme yapabilir miyim?**	*boo <u>kreh</u>•dee kahr•<u>tih</u> ee•<u>leh</u> ur•deh•meh yah•pah•bee•<u>leer</u> mee•yeem*
I have insurance.	**Sigortam var.**	*see•gohr•<u>tahm</u> vahr*
Can I have a receipt for my insurance?	**Sigorta için fiş alabilir miyim?**	*see•gohr•tah ee•cheen feesh ah•lah•bee•leer mee•yeem*

ESSENTIAL

Where's the nearest pharmacy [chemist]?	**En yakın eczane nerede?** _ehn yah·kihn ehj·zah·neh neh·reh·deh_
What time does the pharmacy open/close [chemist]?	**Eczane ne zaman açılıyor/kapanıyor?** _ehj·zah·neh neh zah·mahn ah·chih·lih·yohr/ kah·pah·nih·yohr_
What would you recommend for…?	**…için ne önerirdiniz?** _…ee·cheen neh ur·neh·reer·dee·neez_
How much should I take?	**Ne kadar almalıyım?** _neh kah·dahr ahl·mah·lih·yihm_
Can you fill [make up] this prescription for me?	**Bana bu reçeteyi hazırlar mısınız?** _bah·nah boo reh·cheh·teh·yee hah·zihr·lahr mih·sih·nihz_
I'm allergic to…	**…alerjim var.** _…ah·lehr·jeem vahr_

In Turkey, the **eczane** (pharmacy) fills medical prescriptions and sells non-prescription drugs as well as cosmetics. Regular hours are generally Monday to Saturday from 9:00 a.m. to 7:00 p.m. At other times, pharmacies work on a rotating schedule. Check the store window to find the closest **nöbetçi eczane** (all-night pharmacy).

What to Take

How much should I take?	**Ne kadar almalıyım?** _neh kah•dahr ahl•mah•<u>lih</u>•yihm_
How often?	**Günde kaç defa almalıyım?** _gyun•<u>deh</u> <u>kahch</u> deh•fah ahl•mah•<u>lih</u>•yihm_
Is it suitable for children?	**Çocuklar için uygun mu?** _choh•jook•<u>lahr</u> ee•cheen ooy•<u>goon</u> moo_
I'm taking...	**...alıyorum.** _...ah•<u>lih</u>•yoh•room_
Are there side effects?	**Yan etkisi var mı?** _<u>yahn</u> eht•kee•<u>see</u> <u>vahr</u> mih_
I'd like some medicine for...	**...için bir ilaç istiyorum.** _...ee•cheen beer ee•<u>lahch</u> ees•<u>tee</u>•yoh•room_
a cold	**Soğuk algınlığı** _soh•<u>ook</u> ahl•gihn•lih•<u>ih</u>_
a cough	**Öksürük** _urk•syu•<u>ryuk</u>_
diarrhea	**İshal** _ees•<u>hahl</u>_
a headache	**Baş ağrısı** _bahs ah•rih•sih_
insect bites	**Böcek sokması** _bur•<u>jehk</u> sohk•mah•<u>sih</u>_
motion sickness	**Yol tutması** _yohl toot•mah•<u>sih</u>_
a sore throat	**Boğaz ağrısı** _boh•<u>ahz</u> **ah**•rih•sih_

sunburn	**Güneş yanığı**	gyu·*nehsh* yah·nih·ih
a toothache	**Diş ağrısı**	deesh ah·rih·sih
an upset stomach	**Mide bozukluğu**	mee·*deh* boh·zook·loo·*oo*

YOU MAY SEE...

GÜNDE BİR/ÜÇ KERE	once/three times a day
TABLET	tablet
DAMLA	drop
ÇAY KAŞIĞI	teaspoon
YEMEKDEN ÖNCE	before meals
YEMEKDEN SONRA	after meals
YEMEKLERLE BİRLİKTE	with meals
AÇ KARNINA	on an empty stomach
BÜTÜN YUTUN	swallow whole
UYKUYA YOL AÇABİLİR	may cause drowsiness
İÇİLMEZ	for external use only

Basic Supplies

I'd like...	**...istiyorum.**	... ees·*tee*·yoh·room
acetaminophen [paracetamol]	**Parasetamol**	pah·rah·*seh*·tah·*mohl*
antiseptic cream	**Antiseptik krem**	ahn·tee·sehp·*teek* krehm
aspirin	**Aspirin**	ahs·pee·*reen*
bandages [plasters]	**Bandaj**	bahn·*dahj*
a comb	**Tarak**	tah·*rahk*
condoms	**Prezervatif**	preh·zehr·vah·*teef*
contact lens solution	**Kontakt lens solüsyonu**	kohn·*tahkt* lehns soh·lyus·yoh·*noo*
deodorant	**Deodorant**	deh·oh·doh·*rahnt*

168

a hairbrush	**Saç fırçası** _sahch_ fihr·chah·sih
hair spray	**Saç spreyi** _sahch_ spreh·yee
ibuprofen	**Ibuprofen** ee·_boop_·roh·_fehn_
insect repellent	**Böcek kovucu** bur·_jek_ koh·voo·joo
a nail file	**Tırnak törpüsü** tihr·_nahk_ turr·pyu·_syu_
a (disposable) razor	**(Tek kullanımlık) Jilet** (_tehk_ kool·lah·nihm·_lihk_) jee·_leht_
razor blades	**Jilet** jee·_leht_
sanitary napkins [pads]	**Âdet bezi** ah·_deht_ beh·_zee_
shampoo/conditioner	**Şampuan/Saç kremi** shahm·poo·_ahn_/_sahch_ kreh·mee
soap	**Sabun** sah·_boon_
sunscreen	**Güneş geçirmez krem** gyu·_nehsh_ geh·cheer·_mehz_ krehm
tampons	**Tampon** tahm·_pohn_
tissues	**Kağıt mendil** kah·_iht_ mehn·_deel_
toilet paper	**Tuvalet kağıdı** too·_vah_·leht kah·_ih_·dih
a toothbrush	**Diş fırçası** _deesh_ fihr·çah·_sih_
toothpaste	**Diş macunu** _deesh_ mah·joo·noo

For Baby Essentials, see page 151.

Grammar

Regular Verbs

Turkish verbs use a stem with suffixes that change according to what tense (present, past, future) and person they indicate. The stem of the verb can be found by removing **mak** or **mek** from the infinitive of the verb, e.g. the stem of **gezmek** (to travel) is **gez**; the stem of **açmak** (to open) is **aç.** The past tense has the suffix **–d–** , and the future, the suffix **–ecek–** .

GEZMEK (to travel)		Present	Past	Future
I	**ben**	gez**erim**	gez**dim**	gez**eceğim**
you (sing., inf.)	**sen**	gez**ersin**	gez**din**	gez**eceksin**
he/she/it	**o**	gez**er**	gez**di**	gez**ecek**
we	**biz**	gez**eriz**	gez**dik**	gez**eceğiz**
you (pl./form.)	**siz**	gez**ersiniz**	gez**diniz**	gez**eceksiniz**
they	**onlar**	gez**erler**	gez**diler**	gez**ecekler**

To form the present continuous tense (which can also be used to express the future tense), the suffix **-iyor** is added to the stem, followed by the endings for each person, i.e. **-um**, **-un**, etc. (see below).

GEZMEK (to travel)		Present continuous	Past	Future
I	**ben**	gez**iyorum**	gez**iyordum**	gez**iyor olacağım**
you (sing., inf.)	**sen**	gez**iyorsun**	gez**iyordun**	gez**iyor olacaksın**
he/she/it	**o**	gez**iyor**	gez**iyordu**	gez**iyor olacak**
we	**biz**	gez**iyoruz**	gez**iyorduk**	gez**iyor olacağız**
you (pl./form.)	**siz**	gez**iyorsunuz**	gez**iyordunuz**	gez**iyor olacaksınız**
they	**onlar**	gez**iyorlar**	gez**iyorlardı**	gez**iyor olacaklar**

Irregular Verbs

Turkish is rather remarkable among living languages in having a highly regular verb conjugation system. A minor irregularity is found in thirteen verbs where the present general takes a vowel-harmony congruent vowel after the root that is in the **i/ü** series, rather than the **a/e** series, which is the standard. These are used regularly on a day-to-day nasis and are best learned by heart.

Infinitive	Present Simple	
almak	**alır**	to take/get
bulmak	**bulur**	to find
durmak	**durur**	to stop/to halt
kalmak	**kalır**	to remain/to stay
olmak	**olur**	to be/to become
sanmak	**sanır**	to suppose
varmak	**varır**	to arrive
vurmak	**vurur**	to strike/to hit
bilmek	**bilir**	to know how to
gelmek	**gelir**	to come
görmek	**görür**	to see
ölmek	**ölür**	to die
vermek	**verir**	to give

The rich system of suffixes that are added at the end of verb stems to express tense, person and manner is remarkably regular and uniform in Turkish.

To express the English 'have/has,' you use the word with its possessive ending, followed by the word **-var** meaning 'exists':

I have a car.

Arabam var.

(literally, 'my car exists')

He/She has a bicycle.

Bisikleti var.

(literally, 'his/her bicycle exists')

To say 'don't/doesn't have' the word **yok** is used instead of var:

I don't have a ticket.	**Biletim yok.**
	(literally, 'my ticket exists-not')
He/She doesn't have any money.	**Parası yok.**
	(literally, 'his/her money exists-not')

Word Order

Standard word order in Turkish is subject-object-verb. For instance:

Murat kedileri gördü. Murat saw the cats.

Murat=subject, kedileri=object, gördü=verb.

Questions are formed either with question words:

ne	what
kim	who
nerede	where
nasıl	how
niçin	why

Or, the question particle **mi** is appended after the word that is the focus of the question:

Murat kedileri gördü mü?	Did Murat see the cats?
Murat kedileri mi gördü?	Did Murat see the cats?
Murat mı kedileri gördü?	Was it Murat who saw the cats?

Negations

The letter **–m–** , added between the verb stem and what follows, indicates negation. Some examples:

He/She travels.	**Gezer.**	He/She does not travel.	**Gezmez.**
He/She is traveling.	**Geziyor.**	He/She is not traveling.	**Gezmiyor.**

Imperatives

The imperative for second person singular is simply the verbal stem. The negative imperative is the same with the –m– suffix.

Come! (one person)	**Gel!**
Don't come! (one person)	**Gelme!**

The positive and negative imperatives for second person plural or formal are the same pair, with the plural suffix:

Come! (several persons)	**Gelin!**
Don't come! (several persons)	**Gelmeyin!**

Nouns & Articles

Nouns in Turkish change their ending according to their function in a sentence. These grammatical case endings are themselves subject to change due to vowel harmony. For beginners, it is often difficult to separate the case endings from the other suffixes added to a word and, therefore, it is better to learn words within a complete phrase.

Nouns do not have grammatical gender. The indefinite demonstrative article **bir** (literally, 'one') corresponds closely to the English 'a/an', however there is no definite article corresponding to the English 'the'. This article is generally conveyed by the demonstrative adjectives **bu/şu** (this) and **o** (that).

Adjectives

Adjectives come before the noun, and there are no case or singular/plural endings on them:

uzun yol	long road
uzun yollar	long roads
Uzun yoldan geldim.	I arrived from a long trip.
	(Literally: I arrived from a long road.)

Pronouns

The challenge for English speakers is to know when to use **sen** and **siz**, both of which are 'you' in English. It is clear that a group of people must be addressed with **siz**, the second person plural pronoun. However, this same pronoun, like in some other languages, is used as a respectful form of address for unfamiliar, elderly or hierarchically higher individuals. For the tourist, it is safe to address people with **siz**, until familiarity develops or all agree to use the less formal **sen**. The latter form, **sen**, is the correct form to use among family members, good friends and with children.

I	**ben**
you (sing., inf.)	**sen**
he/she/it	**o**
we	**biz**
you (pl./form.)	**siz**
they	**onlar**

Comparatives & Superlatives

The comparative is generally formed with **daha** (more); it precedes the adjective. Example:

büyük	big
daha büyük	bigger

The preferred way for conveying the sense of 'less' is again through the use of **daha** with the adjective that has the opposite meaning.

küçük	small
daha küçük	smaller

The superlative is formed by adding **en** in front of the adjective:

en büyük	the biggest
en küçük	the smallest

Adverbs & Adverbial Expressions

Almost any adjective can be used as an adverb that modifies a verb:

güzel konuştu	he spoke beautifully
yavaş/süratli sürün!	Drive slowly/quickly!

Adverbs precede the verb or the adjective they qualify, and they take no case or singular/plural endings:

hızlı koşmak	to run fast
koyu mavi gözler	intensely blue eyes

Adverbs may be directional or time-related, or they may qualify the verb:

içeri	inside
ileri	forward
erken	early
geç	late
çok	a lot, too much
az	a little, too little
hemen	right away

The ca/ce suffix forms adverbs from adjectives or nouns:

sinsice	sneakily
kahramanca	heroically

Examples with some of the foregoing:

içeri girin!	Go inside!
çok yedim	I ate too much
erken gelin!	Come early!
sinsice yürüyor	he is walking sneakily
hemen yaparlar	They will do it right away

Numbers

ESSENTIAL

0	**sıfır** _sih•fihr_
1	**bir** _beer_
2	**iki** _ee•kee_
3	**üç** _yuch_
4	**dört** _durrt_
5	**beş** _behsh_
6	**altı** _ahl•tih_
7	**yedi** _yeh•dee_
8	**sekiz** _seh•keez_
9	**dokuz** _doh•kooz_
10	**on** _ohn_
11	**on bir** _ohn beer_
12	**on iki** _ohn ee•kee_
13	**on üç** _ohn yuch_
50	**elli** _ehl•lee_
60	**altmış** _ahlt•mihsh_
70	**yetmiş** _yeht•meesh_
80	**seksen** _sehk•sehn_
90	**doksan** _dohk•sahn_
100	**yüz** _yyuz_
101	**yüz bir** _yyuz beer_
200	**ikiyüz** _ee•kee yyuz_
500	**beşyüz** _behsh yyuz_
1,000	**bin** _been_
10,000	**on bin** _ohn been_
1,000,000	**bir milyo** _beer meel•yohn_

Ordinal Numbers

first	**birinci** *bee•reen•jee*
second	**ikinci** *ee•keen•jee*
third	**üçüncü** *yu•chyun•jyu*
fourth	**dördüncü** *durr•dyun•jyu*
fifth	**beşinci** *beh•sheen•jee*
once	**bir kere** *beer keh•reh*
twice	**iki kere** *ee•kee keh•reh*
three times	**üç kere** *yuch keh•reh*

Time

ESSENTIAL

What time is it?	**Saat kaç?** *sah•aht kahch*
It's noon [midday].	**Saat on iki.** *sah•aht on ee•kee*
At midnight.	**Gece yarısı.** *geh•jeh yah•rih•sih*
From nine o'clock to 5 o'clock.	**Saat dokuzdan beşe.** *sah•aht doh•kooz•dahn beh•sheh*
Twenty after [past] four.	**Dördü yirmi geçiyor.** *durr•dyu yeer•mee geh•chee•yohr*
A quarter to nine.	**Dokuza çeyrek var.** *doh•koo•zah chay•rehk vahr*
5:30 a.m./p.m.	**Öğleden önce/sonra beş buçuk.** *ur•leh•dehn urn•jeh/sohn•rah behsh boo•chook*

Days

ESSENTIAL

Monday	**Pazartesi** pah·<u>zahr</u>·teh·see
Tuesday	**Salı** sah·<u>lih</u>
Wednesday	**Çarşamba** chahr·shahm·<u>bah</u>
Thursday	**Perşembe** pehr·shehm·<u>beh</u>
Friday	**Cuma** joo·<u>mah</u>
Saturday	**Cumartesi** joo·<u>mahr</u>·teh·see
Sunday	**Pazar** pa·<u>zar</u>

Dates

yesterday	**dün** dyun
today	**bugün** <u>boo</u>·gyun
tomorrow	**yarın** <u>yah</u>·rihn
day	**gün** gyun
week	**hafta** hahf·tah
month	**ay** ie
year	**yıl** yihl

Turkey follows a day-month-year format instead of the month-day-year format used in the U.S.

For example, July 25, 2008; **25/07/08** = 7/25/2008 in the U.S.

Months

January	**Ocak** oh·<u>jahk</u>
February	**Şubat** shoo·<u>baht</u>
March	**Mart** mahrt
April	**Nisan** nee·<u>sahn</u>
May	**Mayıs** mah·<u>yihs</u>

June	**Haziran** *hah•zee•rahn*
July	**Temmuz** *tehm•mooz*
August	**Ağustos** *ah•oos•tohs*
September	**Eylül** *ay•lyul*
October	**Ekim** *eh•keem*
November	**Kasım** *kah•sihm*
December	**Aralık** *ah•rah•lihk*

Seasons

spring	**ilkbahar** *eelk•bah•hahr*
summer	**yaz** *yahz*
fall [autumn]	**sonbahar** *sohn•bah•hahr*
winter	**kış** *kihsh*

August 30th, Victory Day, memorializes the final victory that brought the War of Independence to an end in 1922. October 29th is the anniversary of the founding of the Turkish Republic in 1923. The Festival of Sweetmeats and the Festival of Sacrifice are Muslim holidays whose dates are based on the lunar calendar, rather than the Gregorian calendar. The Festival of Sweetmeats is a three-holiday to mark the end of the month of Ramadan. The name marks the tradition of visiting friends and family with a gift of 'sweetmeats.'

The Festival of Sacrifice is a four-day holiday that commemorates the willingness of Abraham to sacrifice his son for Allah. It is celebrated by the sacrifice of an animal followed by a family feast and donations of food to the poor.

Holidays

January 1, New Year's Day	**Yılbaşı**
April 23, National Independence and Children's Day	**Ulusal Egemenlik ve Çocuk Bayramı**
May 19, Commemoration of Atatürk's Landing in Samsun and Youth and Sports Day	**Atatürk'ü Anma, Gençlik ve Spor Bayramı**
August 30, National Independence Victory Day	**Zafer Bayramı**
October 29, Republic Day	**Cumhuriyet Bayramı**
Festival of Sweetmeats	**Şeker Bayramı**
Festival of Sacrifice	**Kurban Bayramı**

April 23rd, National Sovereignty and Children's Day, is the anniversary of the opening of the Grand National Assembly, which happened in Ankara in 1920. Traditionally this is a holiday dedicated to children. May 19th, the Commemoration of Atatürk's Landing in Samsun, Youth and Sports Day, commemorates the start of the Turkish War of Independence, which began in 1919. Now this holiday is dedicated to youth and sports.

Conversion Tables

When you know	Multiply by	To find
ounces	28.3	grams
pounds	0.45	kilograms
inches	2.54	centimeters
feet	0.3	meters
miles	1.61	kilometers
square inches	6.45	sq. centimeters
square feet	0.09	sq. meters
square miles	2.59	sq. kilometers
pints (U.S./Brit)	0.47/0.56	liters
gallons (U.S./Brit)	3.8/4.5	liters
Fahrenheit	5/9, after 32	Centigrade
Centigrade	9/5, then +32	Fahrenheit

Kilometers to Miles Conversions	
1 km	0.62 miles
5 km	3.1 miles
10 km	6.2 miles
50 km	31 miles
100 km	62 miles

Measurement		
1 gram	**gram** *grahm*	= 0.035 oz.
1 kilogram (kg)	**kilogram** *kee·loh·grahm*	= 2.2 lb
1 liter (l)	**litre** *leet·reh*	= 1.06 U.S./ 0.88 Brit. quarts
1 centimeter (cm)	**santimetre** *sahn·tee·meht·reh*	= 0.4 inch
1 meter (m)	**metre** *meht·reh*	= 3.28 feet
1 kilometer (km)	**kilometer** *kee·loh·meht·reh*	= 0.62 mile

Temperature

-40°C – -40°F	**-1°C** – 30°F	**20°C** – 68°F
-30°C – -22°F	**0°C** – 32°F	**25°C** – 77°F
-20°C – -4°F	**5°C** – 41°F	**30°C** – 86°F
-10°C – 14°F	**10°C** – 50°F	**35°C** – 95°F
-5°C – 23°F	**15°C** – 59°F	

Oven Temperature

100°C – 212°F	**177°C** – 350°F
121°C – 250°F	**204°C** – 400°F
149°C – 300°F	**260°C** – 500°F

Dictionary

English–Turkish

A

abroad *adv* yurtdışı
accept *v* kabul etmek
accident kaza
accompany *v* eşlik etmek
acetaminophen parasetamol
acne sivilce
adapter adaptör
address adres
after sonra
air conditioner klima
air sickness bag sıhhi torba
airmail uçak ile
airport *n* havaalanı
aisle seat koridor kenarı koltuk
alarm clock çalar saat
all hepsi
allergy alerji
allow *v* izin vermek
allowance (customs) gümrüksüz
  geçebilecek miktar
almost neredeyse
alone yalnız
already zaten
also ayrıca

alter *v* değiştirmek
alternate route alternatif yol
aluminum foil alimünyum kağıtı
always her zaman
amazing hayret verici
ambassador elçi
ambulance ambülans
American *adj* Amerikan; *n* Amerikalı
amount (money) tutar
amusement park oyun parkı
animal hayvan
another başka bir
antacid mide asidine karşı ilaç
antibiotics antibiyotik
antifreeze antifriz
antique (object) antika
antiseptic *adj* antiseptik
antiseptic cream antiseptik krem
anyone biri
apartment apartman dairesi
apologize *v* özür dilemek
appetite *n* iştah
appointment randevu
April Nisan
area code alan kodu

| **adj** adjective | **BE** British English | **v** verb |
| **adv** adverb | **n** noun | |

arcade oyun salonu

around (place) yakınları; **(time)** civarında

arrival (terminal) variş

arrive *v* varmak

art gallery sanat galerisi

arthritis *n* arterit

ask istemek

aspirin aspirin

assistance yardım

asthma astım

ATM paramatik

attack saldırı

attractive cazip

audio guide teybe alınmış rehber

August Ağustos

Australia Avustralya

authenticity hakikilik

automatic car otomatik araba

autumn [BE] sonbahar

B

baby bebek

baby bottle biberon

baby food bebek maması

baby wipes bebek mendili

babysitter çocuk bakıcısı

back (part of body) sırt

backpack sırt çanta

backache sırt ağrısı

bad kötü

bag çanta

baggage [BE] bavul

baggage cart alış veriş arabası

baggage check emanet

baggage claim bavul teslim bandi

baggage trolley [BE] alış veriş arabası

ball top

bandage bandaj

bank banka

bar bar

basket sepet

basketball basketbol

basketball game basketbol maçı

bathroom tuvalet

battery (vehicle) akü; **(radio, watch)** pil

battle site savaş meydanı

be *v* olmak

beach plaj

beautiful *adj* güzel

bed yatak

before önce

begin *v* başlamak

behind arkasında

belt kemer

bet *n* bahis

between (time) arasında

bicycle bisiklet

big büyük

bikini bikini

bill [BE] fatura; **(receipt at restaurant)** hesap
birthday doğum günü
bite (insect) sokmak
black *adj* siyah
blanket battaniye
blister su toplanması
blood pressure tansiyon
blouse bluz
blue mavi
boat trip tekne gezisi
book *n* kitap
book store kitapçı
boots bot; **(sport)** çizme
boring *adj* sıkıcı
botanical garden botanik bahçesi
bottle şişe
bottle opener şişe açacağı
box kutu
boxing match boks maçı
boy erkek çocuk
boyfriend erkek arkadaş
bra sütyen
break *v* kırmak
breast meme
breathe *v* nefes almak
bridge köprü
briefs külot
bring *v* getirmek
Britain Britanya
British Britanyalı

brooch broş
broom süpürge
bus otobüs
bus station otobüs garajı
bus stop otobüs durağı
business iş
business center iş merkezi
busy kalabalık
but ama
buy *v* satın almak

C

cable car teleferik
cafe kafe
calendar takvim
call *v* çağırmak; **(telephone)** aramak
call collect karşı tarafa ödetmek
camera fotoğraf makinesi
camp *v* kamp yapmak
campsite *n* kamp alanı
can opener konserve açacağı
Canada Kanada
cancel *v* iptal etmek
car araba; **(train compartment)** vagon
car park [BE] otopark
car rental araba kiralama
car seat araba koltuğu
carafe *n* sürahi
carpet (rug) halı

carry-on el çantası

carton kutu

cash para; nakit

cash desk [BE] kasa

cashier kasa

casino kumarhane

castle kale

cat kedi

catch *v* **(bus)** yetişmek

cathedral katedral

cave mağara

cell phone cep telefonu

certificate belge

change *n* **(coins)** bozuk para; *v* **(alter)** değiştirmek; **(bus, train)** aktarma yapmak; **(money)** bozdurmak

changing facilities bebeğin altını değiştirecek yer

charcoal odun kömürü

charge ücret

cheap ucuz

check fatura; **(receipt at restaurant)** hesap

check in *v* check-in yaptırmak

check-in desk uçuş kaydi masası

check out (hotel) otelden ayrılmak

checking account cari hesap

chemist [BE] eczane

chest pain göğüs ağrısı

child çocuk

child seat çocuk sandalyesi

child's cot [BE] çocuk yatağı

church kilise

cigar puro

cigarette sigara

cinema [BE] sinema

classical music klasik müzik

clean *adj* temiz; *v* temizlemek

cleaning supplies temizlik maddeleri

clear silmek

cliff uçurum

cling film [BE] plastik ambalaj kağıdı

clock saat

close (near) yakın; *v* kapanmak

clothing store elbise mağazası

club (golf) sopa

coach (long-distance bus) şehirlerarası otobüs

coat palto

code (area) kod

coin madeni para

cold *n* **(flu)** soğuk algınlığı; *adj* **(temperature)** soğuk

colleague meslektaş

collect *v* almak

color renk

comb tarak

come *v* gelmek

commission komisyon

company (business) şirket; **(companionship)** arkadaşlık
computer bilgisayar
concert konser
concert hall konser salonu
conditioner saç kremi
condom prezervatif
conference konferans
confirm v teyit etmek
consulate konsolosluk
contact v bağlantı kurmak
contact lens kontak lens
contain v içermek
convention hall kongre salonu
cook ahçı
cooking facility pişirme olanağı; mutfak
copper bakır
corkscrew şarap açacağı
cost v tutmak
cot bebek yatağı
cotton (fabric) pamuklu; **(cotton wool)** pamuk
cough öksürük
country ülke
country code ülke kodu
courier (guide) rehber
cover charge masa ücreti
cramps kramp
credit card kredi kartı
crib çocuk yatağı

cruise n deniz yolculuğu
crystal (quartz) kuartz
cup fincan
currency para birimi
currency exchange office döviz bürosu
current account [BE] cari hesap
curtain perde
customs gümrük
cut kesik
cycling race bisiklet yarışı

D

damage n hasar
dance n dans; v dans etmek
dance club diskotek
dangerous curve tehlikeli kavşak
day gün
deaf sağır
December Aralık
deck chair katlanabilir koltuk
declare v beyan etmek
deep derin
delay gecikme
denim kot kumaşı
dentist diş doktoru
denture protez
deodorant deodoran
depart v (train, bus) kalkmak
department store mağaza
departure gate çıkış kapisi

deposit ön ödeme
desert çöl
detergent deterjan
diabetic (person) şeker hastası
diamond elmas
diaper bebek bezi
diarrhea ishal
dictionary sözlük
die ölmek
diesel dizel
difficult zor
directory (telephone) rehber
dirty kirli
disabled [BE] özürlü
discount indirim
dish (utensil) tabak çanak
dishwasher bulaşık makinesi
dishwashing liquid bulaşık
    deterjanı
disposable razor tek kullanımlık
    jilet
dive *v* dalmak
diving equipment dalış donanımı
divorced boşanmış
do *v* yapmak
doctor doktor
doll bebek
dollar (U.S.) dolar
domestic flight iç hat uçuşu
door kapı
double room çift kişilik oda

downtown area kent merkezi
dress elbise
dress code giyim tarzı
drive *v* seyretmek
driver sürücü
driver's license ehliyet
dry cleaner kuru temizleyici
duty gümrük vergisi
duty-free goods vergisiz eşyalar

E

earache kulak ağrısı
earrings küpe
east doğu
easy *adj* kolay
eat *v* yemek
economy class ekonomi sınıfı
eight sekiz
eighteen on sekiz
eighty seksen
electrical outlet elektrik prizi
electronic elektronik
elevator asansör
eleven on bir
e-mail *n* e-posta; *v* yazmak
e-mail address e-posta adresi
embassy elçilik
emergency acil durum
emergency exit acil çıkış
empty *adj* boş; *v* boşaltmak
end *v* bitmek

England İngiltere
English İngilizce
English-speaking İngilizce konuşan
enjoy v beğenmek
enter v girmek
equipment (sports) donanım
escalator yürüyen merdiven
e-ticket e-bilet
e-ticket check-in e-bilet kaydi
European Union AB
evening gece
excess luggage fazla bavul ağırlığı
exchange v değiştirmek
exchange rate döviz kuru
excursion gezinti
exit n çıkış; v çıkmak
expensive pahalı
expert uzman
express ekspres
extension dahili hat
extra (additional) daha
extra bed ek yatak
eye göz

F

fabric kumaş
facial yüz bakımı
fall sonbahar
family aile
fan (ventilator) vantilatör
far uzak

farm çiftlik
far-sighted yakını görme bozukluğu
fast (ahead) adv ileri; **(speed)** hızlı
fast-food restaurant hazır yemek
  lokantası
fax faks
February Şubat
fee komisyon
feed v yemek vermek
female kadın
ferry vapur
fever ateş
few birkaç tane
field tarla
fifteen on beş
fifty elli
fill v hazırlamak
fill up (car) doldurmak
filling (dental) dolgu
film film
find v bulmak
fine adj iyi
fire yangın
fire door yangin kapisi
fire extinguisher yangın söndürme
  aleti
first class birinci sınıf
fit v **(clothes)** olmak
fitting room soyunma odası
five beş
fix v onarmak

flat *adj* **(shoe)** patlak
flight uçuş
flight number uçuş numarası
floor (level) kat
fly *v* uçmak
folk music halk müziği
food yiyecek
football [BE] futbol
football game [BE] futbol maçı
foreign currency döviz
forest orman
fork çatal
form form
forty kırk
four dört
fourteen on dört
frame (glasses) çerçeve
free (available) boş; **(without charge)** ücretsiz
freezer dondurucu
fresh taze
Friday Cuma
friend arkadaş
full dolu

G

game (match) maç; **(toy)** oyun
garage (parking) garaj; **(repair)** araba tamirhanesi
garbage bag çöp torbası
garden bahçe

gas benzin
gas station benzin istasyonu
gate (airport) biniş kapısı
get *v* **(find)** bulmak
get a refund *v* para geri almak
get off *v* **(bus, etc.)** inmek
get to *v* gitmek
gift shop hediyelik eşya dükkanı
girl kız çocuk
girlfriend kız arkadaş
give *v* vermek
glass bardak
glasses (optical) gözlük
go *v* gitmek
gold altın
golf golf
golf club golf sopası
golf course golf sahası
golf tournament golf turnuvası
good *adj* iyi
green yeşil
grocery store bakkal
ground (earth) zemin
ground-floor room zemin-kat odası
guide (telephone) [BE] rehber; **(tour)** gezi rehberi
guide dog rehber köpeği
guide book rehber kitabı
gym jimnastik
gynecologist kadın hastalıkları uzmanı

H

hair saç
hairbrush saç fırçası
haircut saç tıraşı
hairdresser kuaför
hairspray saç spreyi
half *adj* yarım
hand el
handbag [BE] cüzdan
handicapped özürlü
happen *v* olmak
harbor liman
hard (difficult) zorlu; **(solid)** sert
hat şapka
have *v* sahip olmak
hear *v* duymak
heart kalp
heat *n* ısıtıcı
heater ısıtıcı
heating [BE] *n* ısıtıcı
heavy ağır
helmet kask
help yardım
here burada
high yüksek
highchair yüksek sandalye
highway otoyol
hill tepe
hire [BE] *v* kiralamak
hold on *v* **(wait)** beklemek
holiday [BE] tatil

home ev
horsetrack at yarışı
hospital hastane
hot sıcak
hotel otel
hour saat
house ev
how nasıl
hundred yüz
hungry aç
hurt *v* acımak
husband koca

I

ibuprofen ibuprofen
ice buz
identification kimlik belgesi
ill [BE] hasta
included dahil
incredible inanılmaz
indoor pool kapalı havuz
inexpensive ucuz
infection bulaşma
information bilgi
information desk danışma
   masası
information office danışma bürosu
innocent masum
insect böcek
insect bite böcek sokması
insect repellent böcek kovucu

inside içerde
instant messenger anında
  muhabbet
instruction kullanım talimatı
insurance sigorta
interest (hobby) ilgi alanı
interesting ilginç
intermediate orta seviyede
international flight diş hat uçuşu
internet internet
internet cafe internet kafe
internet service internet hizmeti
interpret tercüme etmek
interpreter tercüman
intersection kavşak
Ireland İrlanda
iron ütü
item eşya
itemized bill dökümlü hesap

J

jacket monta
January Ocak
jazz caz
jeans kot pantalon
jet-ski jet ski
jeweler kuyumcu
jewelry mücevherat
job iş
join v **(accompany)** katılmak; **(to
  get involved)** girmek

July Temmuz
June Haziran

K

key anahtar
key ring anahtarlık
kiddie pool çocuk havuzu
kilometer kilometre
kiss v öpmek
kitchen mutfak
kitchen foil [BE] alimünyum
  kağıtı
know v bilmek

L

lace dantel
lake göl
land v **(airplane)** inmek
large büyük
last adj son; sonuncu; v devam
  etmek
late geç
launderette [BE] çamaşırhane
laundromat çamaşırhane
laundry facility çamaşırhane
lawyer avukat
leather deri
leave v **(depart)** kalkmak; **(deposit)**
  bırakmak; **(go)** gitmek
left (side) sol
leg bacak

lens (camera) objektif; **(glasses)** cam
letter mektup
library kitaplık
life boat cankurtaran sandalı
life jacket can yeleği
lifeguard cankurtaran
lift [BE] asansör
lift pass teleferik pasosu
light n **(electric)** ışık; adj **(not dark)** aydınlık; **(not heavy)** hafif; **(color)** açık; **(on vehicle)** far
light bulb ampul
lighter (cigarette) çakmak
like v beğenmek
line (subway) hat
linen keten
liquor store tekel bayii
lira (Turkish currency, YTL) lira
liter litre
little (small) küçük
live v yaşamak
live music canlı müzik
local yerel
lock kilit
log on v girmek
login giriş
logout n çıkış; v çıkmak
long uzun
look like v benzemek
lose v kaybetmek

love v **(like)** beğenmek; **(somebody)** sevmek
low düşük
low bridge alçak köprü
luggage bavul
luggage cart el arabası
luggage locker bagaj dolapı

M

machine washable makinede yıkanabilir
magazine dergi
magnificent muhteşem
mail mektup
mailbox posta kutusu
main ana; başlıca
make-up n makyaj; v **(a prescription) [BE]** hazırlamak
male (man) erkek
mall alış veriş merkezi
manager müdür
manicure manikür
manual (car) el kitabı
map harita
March Mart
market pazar
mascara rimel
massage masaj
May Mayıs
match (smoking) kibrit; **(sports)** maç

measurement ölçü
medicine (medication) ilaç
medium (size) orta
meet v buluşmak
meeting toplantı
meeting room toplantı odası
message mesaj
microwave mikrodalga
midnight gece yarısı
mistake yanlışlık
mobile phone [BE] cep telefonu
moisturizer (cream)
  nemlendirici
moment an
Monday Pazartesi
money para
month ay
mop yer bezi
moped mopet
mosque cami
motion sickness yol tutması
motorboat motorlu tekne
motorcycle motorsiklet
motorway [BE] otoyol
mountain dağ
mouth ağız
move v taşınmak
movie film
movie theater sinema
movies theater sinema
mugging hırsızlık

museum müze
music müzik

N

nail file tırnak törpüsü
name isim
napkin peçete
nappy [BE] bebek bezi
national ulusal
near yakın
necklace kolye
new yeni
New Zealand Yeni Zelanda
newspaper gazete
newsstand gazete bayii
next (following) bir sonraki
next to yanında
nice iyi
nightclub gece klübü
nine dokuz
nineteen on dokuz
ninety doksan
non-smoking sigara içilmeyen
north kuzey
nose burun
nothing hiçbir şey
notify v bildirmek
November Kasım
novice acemi
number numara
nurse hemşire

O

October Ekim
office ofis
office hours çalışma saatleri
off-licence [BE] tekel bayii
off-peak kalabalık saatler dışında
often sık sık
old (senior) yaşlı; **(thing)** eski
one bir
one way tek yön
one-way ticket sırf gidiş
open *adj* açık; *v* **(store)** açılmak; *v* **(a window)** açmak
opening hours açılış saatleri
opera opera
opposite karşıda; karşısında
optician göz doktoru
orange (color) portakal rengi
order *v* sipariş vermek
outdoor açık havada
outdoor pool açık havuz
outside dışında; dışarda
overlook hakim tepe

P

pacifier emzik
pack *v* hazırlamak
package paket
paddling pool [BE] çocuk havuzu
pain acı
palace saray

pants pantalon
pantyhose tayt
paper towels kağıt havlusu
paracetamol [BE] parasetamol
park park
parking park yeri
parking lot otopark
party (social) parti
pass *v* **(a place)** geçmek
pass through geçmek
passport pasaport
passport control pasaport kontrolu
pastry store pastane
path patika
pay *v* ödemek
payment ödeme
peak tepe
pedestrian crossing yaya geçidi
pediatrician çocuk doktoru
people insanlar
period (menstrual) aybaşı
person kişi
petrol [BE] benzin
petrol station [BE] benzin istasyonu
pewter kurşun-kalay alaşımı
pharmacy eczane
phone *n* telefon; *v* telefon etmek
phone call telefon görüşmesi
phone card telefon kartı
photocopy fotokopi
photograph fotoğraf

phrase book konuşma kılavuzu

pick up v almak

picnic area piknik alanı

piece (item) parça

pill hap; (contraceptive) doğum kontrol hapı

pillow yastık

pillow case yastık kılıfı

PIN pin numarasi

piste [BE] pist

place yer

plane uçak

plaster [BE] bandaj

plastic wrap plastik ambalaj kağıdı

plate tabak

platform [BE] peron

platinum platin

play n (theater) tiyatro oyunu; v (game) oynamak; (music) çalmak

playground çocuk parkı

plunger plançer

pocket cep

pole kayak sopası

point v (to something) göstermek

police polis

police report polis raporu

police station polis karakolu

pond gölcük

pop music pop

port (harbor) liman

post [BE] n posta; v postaya vermek

postbox [BE] posta kutusu

post office [BE] postane

postcard kartpostal

pottery çanak çömlek

pound (sterling) İngiliz sterlini

pregnant hamile

prescription reçete

press v ütülemek

price fiyat

problem soru

program program

purple mor

purpose sebeb

purse cüzdan

push chair [BE] puşet

put v koymak

Q

quarter çeyrek

quiet sessiz

R

racetrack hipodrom

racket (tennis, squash) raket

railway station [BE] tren garı

raincoat yağmurluk

rainy yağmurlu

rap rep

rape tecavüz

rash kaşıntı

razor jilet

razor blades jilet
ready hazır
real (genuine) gerçek; hakiki
receipt fatura; fiş
recommend v önermek
refrigerator buzdolabı
region bölge
regular (gas) normal; **(size)** orta
  boy
religion din
rent v kiralamak
repair v onarmak
repeat v tekrarlamak; tekrar etmek
report v **(crime)** haber vermek
reservation yer ayırtmak
reserve (a table) v ayırtmak
restaurant lokanta
restroom tuvalet
return (ticket) [BE] gidiş dönüş; v
  (come back) dönmek; **(surrender)**
  bırakmak
right (correct) doğru
ring yüzük
river ırmak
road yol
road map yol haritası
robbery soygun
romantic romantik
room oda
room service oda servisi
round (of game) tur

round-trip gidiş dönüş
route yol
rubbish [BE] çöp
rubbish bag [BE] çöp torbası

S

safe n kasa; adj **(not dangerous)**
  güvenli
sales tax KDV
sandals sandalet
sanitary napkin kadın bağı
sanitary pad [BE] kadın bağı
Saturday Cumartesi
sauna sauna
saving (account) tasarruf hesap
scarf eşarp
schedule tarife
scissors makas
Scotland İskoçya
sea deniz
seat (theater, movies) yer; **(train)**
  koltuk
see v görmek; **(witness)** tanık olmak
sell v satmak
seminar seminer
send göndermek
senior citizen yaşlı
separately ayrı ayrı
September Eylül
service (church) ayin; **(to a**
  customer) servis

seven yedi
seventeen on yedi
seventy yetmiş
shampoo şampuan
sheet (bed) çarşaf
ship gemi
shirt (men's) gömlek
shoe ayakkabı
shoe store ayakkabı dükkânı
shopping area alış veriş merkezi
shopping centre [BE] alış veriş merkezi
short kısa
shorts şort
show v göstermek
shower duş
side effect yan etkisi
sick hasta
sightseeing tour tur
silk ipek
silver gümüş
single (ticket) [BE] sırf gidiş
single room tek kişilik oda
sit v oturmak
six altı
sixteen on altı
sixty altmış
size beden
skirt etek
skis kayak
slippers terlik

slow (behind) geri; **(speed)** yavaş
small küçük
smoking sigara içilen
smoking area sigara içilen yer
sneakers lastik ayakkabı
snorkel şnorkel
snorkeling equipment şnorkel takımı
snow n kar; v kar yağmak
snowboard kar kayağı
snowshoe kar ayakkabısı
snowy karlı
soap sabun
soccer futbol
soccer game futbol maçı
sock çorap
socket priz
some bazı
something bir şey
soon yakında
soother [BE] emzik
sore throat boğaz ağrısı
south güney
souvenir hediyelik eşya
souvenir guide hediyelik eşya rehberi
souvenir store hediyelik eşya dükkanı
speak v konuşmak; **(language)** bilmek
special özel

sport spor
sports massage spor masajı
sprain burkulma
spring ilkbahar
square (town) meydan
stadium stadyum
stairs merdivenler
stamp *n* **(postage)** pul; *v*
  mühürletmek
start *v* **(car)** çalıştırmak;
  (commence) başlamak
stay *v* kalmak
steep dik
stomach mide
stomachache mide ağrısı
stop *n* **(bus)** durak; **(subway)** metro
  istasyonu; *v* durmak
store mağaza
store directory mağaza rehberi
store guide [BE] mağaza rehberi
stove fırın
straight ahead doğru ilerde
strange şaşırtıcı
stream dere
strike *v* **(hit)** vurmak
stroller puşet
student öğrenci
study *v* okumak
summer yaz
Sunday Pazar
suppose sanmak

style üslup
subway metro
subway map metro planı
subway station metro
  istasyonu
suggest *v* önermek
suit takım elbise
suitable uygun
sun güneş
sunburn güneş yanığı
sunglasses güneş gözlüğü
sunny güneşli
sunscreen güneş geçirmez krem
sunstroke güneş çarpması
super (petrol) [BE] süper
superb mükemmel
supermarket süpermarket
suppository fitil
surfboard surf tahtası
sweater süveter
sweatshirt sweatshirt
swelling şişlik
swim *v* yüzmek
swimming pool yüzme havuzu
swimming trunks mayo
swimsuit mayo
synagogue havra

T

table masa
tablet tablet

take *v* **(carry)** götürmek;
  (medicine) almak; **(room)** tutmak;
  (time) binmek
take off çıkartmak
talk *v* konuşmak
tampon tampon
taxi taksi
taxi stand taksi durağı
team takım
tell *v* söylemek
ten on
tennis court tenis kortu
tennis match tenis maçı
tent çadır
terminal terminal
terrible berbat; kötü
that o
theft hırsızlık
thermal spring termal kaynağı
thick kalın
thief hırsız
thin ince
thirteen on üç
thirty otuz
this bu
three üç
throat boğaz
Thursday Perşembe
ticket bilet
ticket office bilet gişesi
tie kravat

tights [BE] tayt
time saat
timetable [BE] tarife
tissue kağıt mendil
tobacconist tütüncü
today bugün
toilet [BE] tuvalet
toilet paper tuvalet kağıdı
tomorrow *adv* yarın
too (extreme) çok
too much çok fazla
tooth diş
toothache diş ağrısı
toothbrush diş fırçası
toothpaste diş macunu
tour (sightseeing) tur
tourist turist
tourist office turist danışma bürosu
towel havlu
town şehir; kent
town map kent haritası
town square kasaba meydanı
toy store oyuncakçı
track peron
traditional geleneksel
traffic light trafik ışığı
trail pist
trail map pist haritası
train tren
train station tren garı
trash çöp

travel agency seyahat acentası
travel sickness [BE] yol tutması
traveler's check seyahat çeki
traveller's cheque [BE] seyahat çeki
trim uçlarından alma
trip yolculuk; gezi
trousers [BE] pantalon
try on v (clothes) denemek
T-shirt tişört
Tuesday Salı
tunnel tünel
Turkey Türkiye
Turkish (language) Türkçe; **(nationality)** Türk
turn off v kapatmak
turn on v açmak
TV televizyon
twelve on iki
twenty yirmi
two iki
typical tipik

U

ugly çirkin
umbrella şemsiye
under altında
underground [BE] metro
underground map [BE] metro planı
underground station [BE] metro istasyonu

underpants [BE] külot
understand v anlamak
United Kingdom Birleşik Krallık
United States of America Amerika Birleşik Devletleri
unlimited mileage sınırsız yakıt kullanımı
until kadar
upset stomach mide bozukluğu
urgent acil
use v kullanmak

V

vacation tatil
vacation resort tatil yeri
vacuum cleaner elektrikli süpürge
vaginal infection vajina iltihabı
valley vadi
value değer
VAT [BE] KDV
vegetarian (meal) etsiz; **(person)** vejetaryen
very çok
village köy
vineyard bağ
visa vize
visit n ziyaret; v ziyaret etmek
visiting hours ziyaret saatleri
volleyball voleybol
volleyball game voleybol maçı
vomit v kusmak

W

wait *v* beklemek
waiter garson
waitress garson
wake (someone) uyandırmak
wake-up call arama•uyandırma
walking route yürüyüş yolu
wallet cüzdan
warm ılık
washing machine çamaşır
  makinesi
watch (wrist) kol saati
water su
water skis su kayağı
waterfall şelale
way yol
weather hava
weather forecast hava tahmini
Wednesday Çarşamba
weekend rate hafta sonu fiyatı
west batı
what ne
wheelchair tekerlekli sandalye
wheelchair ramp tekerlekli
  sandalye rampası
when ne zaman
where nerede
who kim
why niçin
wife karı

window (office, apartment)
  pencere
window case vitrin
window seat pencere kenarı koltuk
windsurfer rüzgar sörfçüsü
winery şaraphane
wireless internet kablosuz
  internet
winter kış
withdraw funds çekilen paralar
within (time) içinde
wool yün
work *v* **(function)** çalışmak
wrong yanlış

Y

yield yol vermek
youth hostel gençlik yurdu

Z

zero sıfır
zoo hayvanat bahçesi

A

AB European Union
acemi novice
acı pain
acımak hurt *v*
acil urgent
acil çikiş emergency exit
acil durum emergency
aç hungry
açık open *adj*; light *adj* (color)
açık havada outdoor
açık havuz outdoor pool
açılış saatleri opening hours
açılmak open *v* (store)
açmak open *v* (a window); turn on
adaptör adapter
adres address
ağır heavy
ağız mouth
Ağustos August
ahçı cook
aile family
aktarma yapmak change *v* (bus, train)
akü battery (vehicle)
alan kodu area code
alçak köprü low bridge
alış veriş arabası baggage cart [trolley BE]

alerji allergy
alış veriş merkezi mall [shopping centre BE]; shopping area
alimünyum kağıtı aluminum [kitchen BE] foil
almak collect *v*; pick up; take (medicine)
altı six
altın gold
altında under
alternatif yol alternate route
altmış sixty
ama but
ambülans ambulance
Amerika Birleşik Devletleri United States of America
Amerikalı American *n*
Amerikan American *adj*
ampul light bulb
an moment
ana main
anahtar key
anahtarlık key ring
anında muhabbet instant messenger
anlamak understand *v*
antibiyotik antibiotics
antifriz antifreeze
antika antique (object)

antiseptik antiseptic
antiseptik krem antiseptic cream
apartman dairesi apartment
araba car
araba kiralama car rental
araba koltuğu car seat
araba tamirhanesi garage (repair)
Aralık December
aramak call *v* (telephone)
arama-uyandırma wake-up call
arasında between (time)
arkadaş friend
arkadaşlık company (companionship)
arkasında behind
arterit arthritis
asansör elevator [lift BE]
aspirin aspirin
astım asthma
at yarışı horsetrack
ateş fever
avukat lawyer
Avustralya Australia
ay month
ayakkabı shoe
ayakkabı dükkânı shoe store
aybaşı period (menstrual)
aydınlık period *adj* (not dark)
ayırtmak reserve *v* (a table)
ayrı ayrı separately
ayrıca also
ayin service (church)

B

bacak leg
bagaj dolapı luggage locker
bağ vineyard
bağlantı kurmak contact *v*
bahçe garden
bahis bet *n*
bakır copper
bakkal grocery store
bandaj bandage [plaster BE]
banka bank
bar bar
bardak glass
basketbol basketball
basketbol maçı basketball game
başka bir another
başlamak begin *v*; start (commence)
başlıca main
batı west
battaniye blanket
bavul luggage [baggage BE]
bavul teslim bandi baggage claim
bazı some
bebeğin altını değiştirecek yer changing facilities
bebek baby; doll
bebek bezi diaper [nappy BE]
bebek maması baby food
bebek mendili baby wipes
bebek yatağı cot
beden size

beğenmek enjoy *v*; like *v*; love
beklemek hold on *v*; wait
belge certificate
benzemek look like *v*
benzin gas [petrol BE]
benzin istasyonu gas [petrol BE] station
berbat terrible
beş five
beyan etmek declare *v*
bırakmak return *v* (surrender); leave (deposit)
biberon baby bottle
bikini bikini
bildirmek notify *v*
bilet ticket
bilet gişesi ticket office
bilgi information
bilgisayar computer
bilmek know *v*; speak (language)
biniş kapısı gate (airport)
binmek take *v* (time)
bir one
bir şey something
bir sonraki next (following)
biri anyone
birinci sınıf first class
birkaç tane few
Birleşik Krallık United Kingdom
bisiklet bicycle
bisiklet yarışı cycling race

bitmek end *v*
bluz blouse
boğaz throat
boğaz ağrısı sore throat
boks maçı boxing match
boş free (available); empty
boşaltmak empty *v*
boşanmış divorced
bot boots
botanik bahçesi botanical garden
bozdurmak change *v* (money)
bozuk para change *n* (coins)
böcek insect
böcek kovucu insect repellent
böcek sokması insect bite
bölge region
Britanya Britain
Britanyalı British
broş brooch
bu this
bugün today
bulaşık deterjanı dishwashing liquid
bulaşık makinesi dishwasher
bulaşma infection
bulmak find *v*; get
buluşmak meet *v*
burada here
burkulma sprain
burun nose
buz ice

buzdolabı refrigerator
büyük big; large

C

cam glasses
cami mosque
can yeleği life jacket
cankurtaran lifeguard
cankurtaran sandalı life boat
canlı müzik live music
cari hesap checking [current BE] account
caz jazz
cazip attractive
cep pocket
cep telefonu cell [mobile BE] phone
check-in yaptırmak check in v
civarında around (time)
Cuma Friday
Cumartesi Saturday
cüzdan purse [handbag BE]; wallet

Ç

çadır tent
çağırmak call v
çakmak lighter (cigarette)
çalar saat alarm clock
çalışma saatleri office hours
çalışmak work v (function)
çalıştırmak start v (car)
çalmak play v (music)

çamaşır makinesi washing machine
çamaşırhane laundromat [launderette BE]; laundry facility
çanak çömlek pottery
çanta bag
çarşaf sheet (bed)
Çarşamba Wednesday
çatal fork
çekilen paralar withdraw funds
çerçeve frame (glasses)
çeyrek quarter
çıkartmak take off
çıkış exit n; logout
çıkış kapisi departure gate
çıkmak exit v; logout
çift kişilik oda double room
çiftlik farm
çirkin ugly
çizme boots (sport)
çocuk child
çocuk bakıcısı babysitter
çocuk doktoru pediatrician
çocuk havuzu kiddie [paddling BE] pool
çocuk parkı playground
çocuk sandalyesi child seat
çocuk yatağı crib [child's cot BE]
çok too (extreme); very
çok fazla too much
çorap sock

çöl desert
çöp trash [rubbish BE]
çöp torbası garbage [rubbish BE]
   bag

D

dağ mountain
daha extra (additional)
dahil included
dahili hat extension
dalış donanımı diving equipment
dalmak dive v
danışma bürosu information
   office
danışma masası information desk
dans dance n
dans etmek dance v
dantel lace
değer value
değiştirmek change v (alter); alter;
   exchange
denemek try on v (clothes)
deniz sea
deniz yolculuğu cruise n
deodoran deodorant
dere stream
dergi magazine
deri leather
derin deep
deterjan detergent
devam etmek last v

dışarda outside
dışında outside
dik steep
din religion
diş tooth
diş ağrısı toothache
diş doktoru dentist
diş fırçası toothbrush
diş hat uçuşu international flight
diş macunu toothpaste
diskotek dance club
dizel diesel
doğru right (correct)
doğru ilerde straight ahead
doğu east
doğum günü birthday
doğum kontrol hapı pill
   (contraceptive)
doksan ninety
doktor doctor
dokuz nine
dolar dollar (U.S.)
doldurmak fill up (car)
dolgu filling (dental)
dolu full
donanım equipment (sports)
dondurucu freezer
dökümlü hesap itemized bill
dönmek return v (come back)
dört four
döviz foreign currency

döviz bürosu currency exchange office
döviz kuru exchange rate
durak stop *n* (bus)
durmak stop *v*
duş shower
duymak hear *v*
düşük low

E

e-bilet e-ticket
e-bilet kaydi e-ticket check-in
eczane pharmacy [chemist BE]
ehliyet driver's license
ek yatak extra bed
Ekim October
ekonomi sınıfı economy class
ekspres express
el hand
el arabası luggage cart [trolley BE]
el çantası carry-on
el kitabı manual (car)
elbise dress
elbise mağazası clothing store
elçi ambassador
elçilik embassy
elektrik prizi electrical outlet
elektrikli süpürge vacuum cleaner
elektronik electronic
elli fifty

elmas diamond
emanet baggage check
emzik pacifier [soother BE]
e-posta e-mail *n*
e-posta adresi e-mail address
erkek male (man)
erkek arkadaş boyfriend
erkek çocuk boy
eski old (thing)
eşarp scarf
eşlik etmek accompany *v*
eşya item
etek skirt
etsiz vegetarian (meal)
ev home; house
Eylül September

F

faks fax
far light *adj* (on vehicle)
fatura receipt [bill BE]
fazla bavul ağırlığı excess luggage
fırın stove
film film; movie
fincan cup
fiş receipt
fitil suppository
fiyat price
form form
fotoğraf photograph

fotoğraf makinesi camera
fotokopi photocopy
futbol soccer [football BE]
futbol maçı soccer [football BE] game

G

garaj garage (parking)
garson waiter; waitress
gazete newspaper
gazete bayii newsstand
gece evening
gece klübü nightclub
gece yarısı midnight
gecikme delay
geç late
geçmek pass v (a place); pass through
geleneksel traditional
gelmek come v
gemi ship
gençlik yurdu youth hostel
gerçek real (genuine)
geri slow (behind)
getirmek bring v
gezi trip
gezi rehberi guide (tour)
gezinti excursion
gidiş dönüş round-trip [return BE] (ticket)
giriş login

girmek enter v; log on; join (to get involved); get to; go; leave (go)
giyim tarzı dress code
golf golf
golf sahası golf course
golf sopası golf club
golf turnuvası golf tournament
göğüs ağrısı chest pain
göl lake
gölcük pond
gömlek shirt (men's)
göndermek send v
görmek see v
göstermek point v (to something); show
götürmek take v (carry)
göz eye
göz doktoru optician
gözlük glasses (optical)
gümrük customs
gümrük vergisi duty
gümrüksüz geçebilecek miktar allowance (customs)
gümüş silver
gün day
güneş sun
güneş çarpması sunstroke
güneş geçirmez krem sunscreen
güneş gözlüğü sunglasses
güneş yanığı sunburn
güneşli sunny

güney south
güvenli safe *adj* (not dangerous)
güzel beautiful

H

haber vermek report *v* (crime)
hafif light *adj* (not heavy)
hafta sonu fiyatı weekend rate
hakiki real (genuine)
hakikilik authenticity
hakim tepe overlook
halı carpet (rug)
halk müziği folk music
hamile pregnant
hap pill
harita map
hasar damage *n*
hasta sick [ill BE]
hastane hospital
hat line (subway)
hava weather
hava tahmini weather forecast
havaalanı airport
havlu towel
havra synagogue
hayret verici amazing
hayvan animal
hayvanat bahçesi zoo
hazır ready
hazır yemek lokantası fast-food
  restaurant

hazırlamak fill [make-up BE] (a
  prescription) *v*; pack
Haziran June
hediyelik eşya souvenir
hediyelik eşya dükkânı gift shop;
  souvenir store
hediyelik eşya rehberi souvenir
  guide
hemşire nurse
hepsi all
her zaman always
hesap check (receipt at restaurant,
  etc.)
hırsız thief
hırsızlık mugging; theft
hızlı fast (speed)
hiçbir şey nothing
hipodrom racetrack

I

ılık warm
ırmak river
ısıtıcı heat *n*; heater [heating BE]
ışık light *n* (electric)

i

ibuprofen ibuprofen
iç hat uçuşu domestic flight
içerde inside
içermek contain *v*
içinde within (time)

iki two
ilaç medicine (medication)
ileri fast (ahead)
ilgi alanı interest (hobby)
ilginç interesting
ilkbahar spring
inanılmaz incredible
ince thin
indirim discount
İngiliz sterlini pound (sterling)
İngilizce English
İngilizce konuşan English-speaking
İngiltere England
inmek get off *v* (bus); land
  (airplane)
insanlar people
internet internet
internet hizmeti internet service
internet kafe internet cafe
ipek silk
iptal etmek cancel *v*
İrlanda Ireland
ishal diarrhea
isim name
İskoçya Scotland
istemek ask
iş business; job
iş merkezi business center
iştah appetite
iyi fine *adj*; good; nice
izin vermek allow

J

jet ski jet-ski
jilet razor; razor blades
jimnastik gym

K

kablosuz internet wireless
  internet
kabul etmek accept *v*
kadar until
kadın female
kadın bağı sanitary napkin [pad
  BE]
kadın hastalıkları uzmanı
  gynecologist
kafe cafe
kağıt havlusu paper towels
kağıt mendil tissue
kalabalık busy
kalabalık saatler dışında off-
  peak
kale castle
kalın thick
kalkmak depart *v* (train, bus); leave
  (depart)
kalmak stay *v*
kalp heart
kamp alanı campsite
kamp yapmak camp *v*
Kanada Canada
kapalı havuz indoor pool

kapanmak close v; turn off
kapı door
kar snow n
kar ayakkabısı snowshoe
kar kayağı snowboard
kar yağmak snow v
karı wife
karlı snowy
karşı tarafa ödetmek call collect
karşıda opposite
karşısında opposite
kartpostal postcard
kasa cashier [cash desk BE]; safe
kasaba meydanı town square
Kasım November
kask helmet
kaşıntı rash
kat floor (level)
katedral cathedral
katılmak join v (accompany)
katlanabilir koltuk deck chair
kavşak intersection
kayak skis
kayak sopası pole
kaybetmek lose v
kaza accident
KDV sales tax [VAT BE]
kedi cat
kemer belt
kent town
kent haritası town map

kent merkezi downtown area
kesik cut
keten linen
kırk forty
kırmak break v
kısa short
kış winter
kız arkadaş girlfriend
kız çocuk girl
kibrit match (smoking)
kilise church
kilit lock
kilometre kilometer
kim who
kimlik belgesi identification
kiralamak rent [hire BE] v
kirli dirty
kişi person
kitap book n
kitapçı bookstore
kitaplık library
klasik müzik classical music
klima air conditioner
koca husband
kod code (area)
kol saati watch (wrist)
kolay easy
koltuk seat (train)
kolye necklace
komisyon commission; fee
konferans conference

kongre salonu convention hall
konser concert
konser salonu concert hall
konserve açacağı can opener
konsolosluk consulate
kontak lens contact lens
konuşma kılavuzu phrase book
konuşmak talk *v*; speak
koridor kenarı koltuk aisle seat
kot kumaşı denim
kot pantalon jeans
koymak put *v*
köprü bridge
kötü terrible (weather); bad
köy village
kramp cramps
kravat tie
kredi kartı credit card
kuaför hairdresser
kuartz crystal (quartz)
kulak ağrısı earache
kullanım talimatı instruction
kullanmak use *v*
kumarhane casino
kumaş fabric
kurşun-kalay alaşımı pewter
kuru temizleyici dry cleaner
kusmak vomit *v*
kutu box; carton
kuyumcu jeweler
kuzey north

küçük little; small
külot briefs [underpants BE]
küpe earrings

L

lastik ayakkabı sneakers
liman harbor; port
lira (Turkish currency, YTL) lira
litre liter
lokanta restaurant

M

maç match (sports); game (match)
madeni para coin
mağara cave
mağaza store; department store
mağaza rehberi store directory
  [guide BE]
makas scissors
makinede yıkanabilir machine
  washable
makyaj make-up *n*
manikür manicure
Mart March
masa table
masa ücreti cover charge
masaj massage
masum innocent
mavi blue
Mayıs May
mayo swimming trunks; swimsuit

mektup letter; mail

meme breast

merdivenler stairs

mesaj message

meslektaş colleague

metro subway [underground BE]

metro istasyonu subway [underground] stop; subway [underground BE] station

metro planı subway [underground BE] map

meydan square (town)

mide stomach

mide ağrısı stomachache

mide asidine karşı ilaç antacid

mide bozukluğu upset stomach

mikrodalga microwave

monta jacket

mopet moped

mor purple

motorlu tekne motorboat

motorsiklet motorcycle

muhteşem magnificent

mutfak kitchen; cooking facility

mücevherat jewelry

müdür manager

mühürletmek stamp v

mükemmel superb

müze museum

müzik music

N

nakit cash n

nasıl how

ne what

ne zaman when

nefes almak breathe v

nemlendirici moisturizer (cream)

nerede where

neredeyse almost

niçin why

Nisan April

normal regular (gas)

numara number

O

o that

objektif lens (camera)

Ocak January

oda room

oda servisi room service

odun kömürü charcoal

ofis office

okumak study v

olmak be v; fit (clothes); happen

on ten

on altı sixteen

on beş fifteen

on bir eleven

on dokuz nineteen

on dört fourteen

on iki twelve

on sekiz eighteen
on üç thirteen
on yedi seventeen
onarmak fix v; repair
opera opera
orman forest
orta medium (size)
orta boy regular (size)
orta seviyede intermediate
otel hotel
otelden ayrılmak check out (hotel)
otobüs bus
otobüs durağı bus stop
otobüs garajı bus station
otomatik araba automatic car
otopark parking lot [car park BE]
otoyol highway [motorway BE]
oturmak sit v
otuz thirty
oynamak play v (game)
oyun game (toy)
oyun parkı amusement park
oyun salonu arcade
oyuncakçı toy store

Ö

ödeme payment
ödemek pay v
öğrenci student
öksürük cough

ölçü measurement
ölmek die
ön ödeme deposit
önce before
önermek recommend v; suggest
öpmek kiss v
özel special
özür dilemek apologize v
özürlü handicapped [disabled BE]

P

pahalı expensive
paket package
palto coat
pamuk cotton (cotton wool)
pamuklu cotton (fabric)
pantalon pants [trousers BE]
para cash n; money
para birimi currency
para geri almak get a refund v
paramatik ATM
parasetamol acetaminophen [paracetamol BE]
parça piece (item)
park park
park yeri parking
parti party (social)
pasaport passport
pasaport kontrolu passport control
pastane pastry store

patika path
patlak *adj* flat (shoe)
pazar market
Pazar Sunday
Pazartesi Monday
peçete napkin
pencere window (office, apartment)
pencere kenarı koltuk window seat
perde curtain
peron track [platform BE]
Perşembe Thursday
piknik alanı picnic area
pil battery (radio, watch)
pin numarası PIN
pişirme olanağı cooking facility
pist trail [piste BE]
pist haritası trail map
plaj beach
plançer plunger
plastik ambalaj kağıdı plastic wrap [cling film BE]
platin platinum
polis police
polis karakolu police station
polis raporu police report
pop pop music
portakal rengi orange (color)
posta mail *n* [post BE]
posta kutusu mailbox [postbox BE]

postane post office
postaya vermek mail *v* [post BE]
prezervatif condom
priz socket
program program
protez denture
pul stamp *n* (postage)
puro cigar
puşet stroller [push chair BE]

R

raket racket (tennis, squash)
randevu appointment
reçete prescription
rehber courier (guide); directory [guide BE] (telephone)
rehber kitabı guide book
rehber köpeği guide dog
renk color
rep rap
rimel mascara
romantik romantic
rüzgar sörfçüsü windsurfer

S

saat clock; hour; time
sabun soap
saç hair
saç fırçası hairbrush
saç kremi conditioner
saç spreyi hairspray

saç tıraşı haircut
sağır deaf
sahip olmak have *v*
saldırı attack
Salı Tuesday
sanat galerisi art gallery
sandalet sandals
sanmak suppose
saray palace
satın almak buy *v*
satmak sell *v*
sauna sauna
savaş meydanı battle site
sebeb purpose
sekiz eight
seksen eighty
seminer seminar
sepet basket
sert hard (solid)
servis service (to customer)
sessiz quiet
sevmek love *v* (somebody)
seyahat acentası travel agency
seyahat çeki traveler's check
   [cheque BE]
seyretmek drive *v*
sıcak hot
sıfır zero
sıhhi torba air sickness bag
sık sık often
sıkıcı boring

sınırsız yakıt kullanımı unlimited
   mileage
sırf gidiş one-way [single BE]
   ticket
sırt back (part of body)
sırt ağrısı backache
sırt çanta backpack
sigara cigarette
sigara içilen smoking
sigara içilen yer smoking area
sigara içilmeyen non-smoking
sigorta insurance
silmek clear
sinema movie theater [cinema BE]
sipariş vermek order *v*
sivilce acne
siyah black
soğuk cold *adj* (temperature)
soğuk algınlığı cold *n* (flu)
sokmak bite (insect)
sol left (side)
son last *adj*
sonbahar fall [autumn BE]
sonra after
sonuncu last *adj*
sopa club (golf)
soru problem
soygun robbery
soyunma odası fitting room
söylemek tell *v*
sözlük dictionary

spor sport
spor masajı sports massage
stadyum stadium
su water
su kayağı water skis
su toplanması blister
surf tahtası surfboard
süper super (gas [petrol BE])
süpermarket supermarket
süpürge broom
sürahi carafe
sürücü driver
sütyen bra
süveter sweater
sweatshirt sweatshirt

Ş

şampuan shampoo
şapka hat
şarap açacağı corkscrew
şaraphane winery
şaşırtıcı strange
şehir town
şehirlerarası otobüs coach (long-distance bus)
şeker hastası diabetic (person)
şelale waterfall
şemsiye umbrella
şirket company (business)
şişe bottle
şişe açacağı bottle opener

şişlik swelling
şnorkel snorkel
şnorkel takımı snorkeling equipment
şort shorts
Şubat February

T

tabak plate
tabak çanak dish (utensil)
tablet tablet
takım team
takım elbise suit
taksi taxi
taksi durağı taxi stand
takvim calendar
tampon tampon
tanık olmak see v (witness)
tansiyon blood pressure
tarak comb
tarife schedule [timetable BE]
tarla field
tasarruf hesap saving (account)
taşınmak move v
tatil vacation [holiday BE]
tatil yeri vacation resort
tayt pantyhose [tights BE]
taze fresh
tecavüz rape
tehlikeli kavşak dangerous curve
tek kişilik oda single room

tek kullanımlık jilet disposable razor
tek yön one way
tekel bayii liquor store [off-licence BE]
tekerlekli sandalye wheelchair
tekerlekli sandalye rampası wheelchair ramp
tekne gezisi boat trip
tekrar etmek repeat *v*
tekrarlamak repeat *v*
teleferik cable car
teleferik pasosu lift pass
telefon phone *n*
telefon etmek phone *v*
telefon görüşmesi phone call
telefon kartı phone card
televizyon TV
temiz clean
temizlemek clean *v*
temizlik maddeleri cleaning supplies
Temmuz July
tenis kortu tennis court
tenis maçı tennis match
tepe hill; peak
tercüman interpreter
tercüme etmek interpret *v*
terlik slippers
termal kaynağı thermal spring
terminal terminal

teybe alınmış rehber audio guide
teyit etmek confirm *v*
tırnak törpüsü nail file
tipik typical
tişört T-shirt
tiyatro oyunu play *n* (theater)
top ball
toplantı meeting
toplantı odası meeting room
trafik ışığı traffic light
tren train
tren garı train [railway BE] station
tur round (of game); sightseeing tour
turist tourist
turist danışma bürosu tourist office
tutar amount (money)
tutmak take *v* (room); cost
tuvalet bathroom; restroom [toilet BE]
tuvalet kağıdı toilet paper
tünel tunnel
Türk Turkish (nationality)
Türkçe Turkish (language)
Türkiye Turkey
tütüncü tobacconist

U

ucuz cheap; inexpensive
uçak plane

uçak ile airmail
uçlarından alma trim
uçmak fly v
uçurum cliff
uçuş flight
uçuş kaydı masası check-in desk
uçuş numarası flight number
ulusal national
uyandırmak wake (someone)
uygun suitable
uzak far
uzman expert
uzun long

Ü

ücret charge
ücretsiz free (without charge)
üç three
ülke country
ülke kodu country code
üslup style
ütü iron
ütülemek press v

V

vadi valley
vagon car (train compartment)
vajina iltihabı vaginal infection
vantilatör fan (ventilator)
vapur ferry
variş arrival (terminal)

varmak arrive v
vejetaryen vegetarian (person)
vergisiz eşyalar duty-free goods
vermek give v
vitrin window (store); window case
vize visa
voleybol volleyball
voleybol maçı volleyball game
vurmak strike v (hit)

Y

yağmurlu rainy
yağmurluk raincoat
yakın near; close (near)
yakında soon
yakını görme bozukluğu far-sighted
yakınları around (place)
yalnız alone
yan etkisi side effect
yangın fire
yangin kapisi fire door
yangın söndürme aleti fire extinguisher
yanında next to
yanlış wrong
yanlışlık mistake
yapmak do v
yardım help; assistance
yarım half adj
yarın tomorrow

yaşamak live v
yaşlı senior citizen; old *adj* (senior)
yastık pillow
yastık kılıfı pillow case
yatak bed
yavaş slow (speed)
yaya geçidi pedestrian crossing
yaz summer
yazmak e-mail v
yedi seven
yemek eat v
yemek vermek feed v
yeni new
Yeni Zelanda New Zealand
yer place; seat (theater, movies)
yer ayırtmak reservation
yer bezi mop
yerel local
yeşil green
yetişmek catch v (bus)
yetmiş seventy
yirmi twenty
yiyecek food
yol road; route; way
yol haritası road map
yol tutması motion [travel BE]
  sickness
yol vermek yield
yolculuk trip
yurtdışı abroad
yüksek high

yüksek sandalye highchair
yün wool
yürüyen merdiven escalator
yürüyüş yolu walking route
yüz hundred
yüz bakımı facial
yüzme havuzu swimming pool
yüzmek swim v
yüzük ring

Z

zaten already
zemin ground (earth)
zemin-kat odası ground-floor
  room
ziyaret visit n
ziyaret etmek visit v
ziyaret saatleri visiting hours
zor difficult
zorlu hard (difficult)

Berlitz®

speaking your language

phrase book & dictionary
phrase book & CD

Available in: Arabic, Cantonese Chinese, Croatian, Czech, Danish, Dutch, English*, Finnish*, French, German, Greek, Hebrew*, Hindi, Hungarian*, Indonesian, Italian, Japanese, Korean, Latin American Spanish, Mandarin Chinese, Mexican Spanish, Norwegian, Polish, Portuguese, Romanian*, Russian, Spanish, Swedish, Thai, Turkish, Vietnamese

*Book only

www.berlitzpublishing.com